WAG to
WARRIOR

Every Woman's Roadmap to
Overcoming Life's Challenges
and Rewriting HER Story

Belinda Coleman

WAG to WARRIOR
Every Woman's Roadmap to Overcoming Life's
Challenges and Rewriting HER Story
© 2025 Ms Belinda S Coleman

ISBN: 9781068444401 Paperback

Published by: Inspired By Publishing

The strategies in this book are presented primarily for enjoyment and educational purposes. Every effort has been made to trace copyright holders and obtain their permission for the use of copyright material.

The author is a licensed professional coach, not a physician, psychotherapist or healthcare professional. The information and resources provided in this book are based on the authors' personal experiences and professional coaching insights. They are not intended as medical or psychological advice. Always consult with a qualified healthcare professional, before making any significant changes to your health or lifestyle. Any outcomes, income statements or other results, are based on the authors' experiences and there is no guarantee that your experience will be the same. There is an inherent risk in any business enterprise or activity, and there is no guarantee that you will have similar results as a result of reading this book. The author assumes no responsibility for any actions you take based on its content.

The author reserves the right to make changes and assumes no responsibility or liability whatsoever on behalf of any purchaser or reader of these materials.

Dedication

For my Sonny, Christy, Faraday and Georgie – you are my world x

Acknowledgements

The creation of this book was a long time coming, but without the support and love of my family and friends, it would not have been possible.

My biggest supporters are my four amazing children, and I'd like to thank them first because they have stood by my side throughout this process, cheering me on every step of the way.

My son, Sonny, whose words of encouragement were invaluable – though amusingly, it wasn't until he read my first chapter that he realised his mother could write! From that moment on, he loved everything I did.

My daughter Christy, on the other hand, took on the role of critic and whip-cracker, having read countless chapters that didn't even make it into the book. She kept me on the straight and narrow and gave me firm but crucial feedback. In my opinion, she should become an editor!

Then there's my daughter Faraday, who sat intently listening as I read her my chapters, depriving her of precious time watching her beloved *Friends* on TV. Her smile, love and her neverending support kept me going.

And last, but by no means least, my daughter Georgie (along with her boyfriend Jack), who kept me supplied with hundreds of cups of tea as I toiled over my laptop. Not a day went by when they weren't plentiful. And as if that weren't enough, Georgie always had a big, fat hug for me, as if to say, "You're doing okay" and, "I'm proud of you."

I also want to thank my late mum Brenda and my stepdad Mike. Without them, I honestly don't know how I would have coped throughout my life and in my marriage. They were there for me, no matter what, and their commitment and dedication got me through both the good times and the bad. They were amazing grandparents to my four children and my brother's three, and their love and support have been such a great example to us all. My mum's legacy lives on in all of us, and I know her love continues to guide me.

Thank you to Jack and Mary, the best grandparents in the world, for their love and encouragement and for being just wonderful. Thank you for the fun, the laughter and the music, for teaching me that kindness goes a long way and that the love of family is the greatest gift of all.

Thank you to my brother Michael and his wife, Sue, who are my biggest inspiration for their unshakable commitment to each other and their family. My brother, despite his illness, always manages to keep smiling and never fails to make me laugh, while Sue has always been loved for her unselfish, kind and caring ways.

I'd like to thank all my friends for their supportive messages and words of encouragement, which kept me going and pushed me to get this done. More than anything, I'm grateful for their understanding when I had to turn down invitations because "I'm working on the book." As much as I hated missing out on the socials, I doubt this book would exist if I'd been out tripping the light fantastic every week!

To my dad, for instilling in me the discipline that has served me well throughout my life. He always believed that self-discipline is the foundation of success. His support over the years in all my endeavours has meant the world to me because he always wanted me to win.

I'd also like to thank my former therapist Vanessa, who has always supported me through thick and thin. Her valuable feedback, kind words and willingness to read this (when the book was, shall we say, a little raw) means more than I can express.

A huge thank you to all at Inspired By Publishing for their patience, especially for the delays on my part (which I'm sure led to a few hair-pulling moments at times) and also for all their hard work in making this a reality.

Lastly, I'd like to mention my beautiful friend Maggie, who is lovingly remembered in Chapter Six. She lost her battle with cancer just before I finished the book, but she always championed me with her kind heart and uplifting words. I was able to read her the chapter before she passed, and I will always cherish that moment. I miss the laughter and our cheese and wine lunches while putting the world to rights. But I know she's still rooting for me.

Each and every one of you has given me strength in ways you may never fully realise. Your love, kindness and unwavering support have carried me through the hardest moments and lifted me higher in the best ones. The gratitude I feel is beyond words, and I hope you know how deeply you are valued. The love reflected here is not just a chapter of my journey; it's the foundation that has helped me stand tall. I couldn't have done this without you, and for that, I am forever grateful.

Preface

As a child, I often sat by the window in class, my mind wandering far beyond the classroom walls. I would dream about the person I would become, the adventures I would have and the places I would explore. My imagination felt infinite, a space where everything was possible, full of desires, hope and excitement. I used to create entire worlds in my mind, worlds where my dreams had no limits.

Imaginative thinking is the soil where our dreams are planted. It's the place where aspirations take root and begin to grow. As children, we naturally inhabit this space. Our imagination knows no boundaries; it doesn't question our worth. But somewhere along the way, life teaches us to play small. We are conditioned to stay within the lines, blend in and suppress the dreams that once set our hearts on fire. It takes just one moment of doubt, one disapproving voice, to make us question the validity of our desires. And when that happens, we learn to push them aside, believing they're not worth pursuing.

I vividly remember one such moment, sitting in my classroom, staring out the window, my mind full of exciting plans. Suddenly, my teacher's voice pierced my thoughts: "Belinda Doherty, stop daydreaming and pay attention." Instantly, I felt myself shrink, sinking lower in my seat, wishing I could disappear. Awkward and embarrassed, I tried to avoid the stares of my classmates as I was jolted back to reality. From that day, a small seed of doubt was planted.

My form teacher even brought it up during parents' evening, mentioning it to my mum as if it was a serious flaw of mine. It felt like a judgement on my character, a message that my natural inclination to dream needed correcting. Yet, despite my efforts to curtail this alleged fault, I was unable to silence my imagination.

This anecdote provides a crucial perspective: early influences can stop you in your tracks. They can become the persistent voice of doubt that follows you into adulthood, convincing you that your dreams are unrealistic, unimportant or mere fantasy. But I realised that daydreaming isn't something to be ashamed of and that it's far more than a distraction. In those moments we escape into our thoughts fueling our creativity and motivation.

Our imagination is where the seeds of ambition take root. It's where it all begins; everything we aspire to, every great idea and every courageous step towards our goals with the simple act of imagining what we could be and what we could achieve. That's where the magic happens, when we let our minds wander and explore the "what ifs" of life.

Just over a year ago, this book was one of those what-ifs. I had wanted to write a book for years, but if anyone had ever told me that I'd have one sitting on the shelves at Waterstones or WH Smith in my latter years, I probably wouldn't have believed them. But now, looking back, the timing really couldn't have been better.

The way I have written this book mirrors the different stages of our lives, starting from childhood all the way to adulthood. My goal is to help you understand how we become entangled in our own melodrama and how we unknowingly let our past experiences dictate the direction of our lives.

This book is about transformation, about awakening to the hidden powers of the mind and mastering our mindset so we no longer fall victim to self-sabotaging patterns. It's about leading with confidence, love, grace and power.

The first half is deeply personal. This is where I share my story and the experiences that shaped my identity. I hope that as you read, you'll gain a deeper understanding of how your own past has influenced you, your beliefs and the way you navigate life.

The second half focuses on the many challenges often faced in our personal lives and explores the obstacles, pressures and expectations that can test us, shake our confidence and hold us back while offering insights and strategies to help you redefine your path.

Writing this book has been both mentally and emotionally challenging at times, but has also been deeply cathartic. Countless hours of dedication, love and passion have gone into its creation. I chose not to work with a ghostwriter or mentor, which, given my ADHD, made the process even more chaotic. Honestly, I must have written 10 different books during the process with all the changes I made – I'm not kidding! The book became my steadfast companion on my ongoing journey of personal growth, and as it evolved, so did I.

The more I poured into its pages, the more open and vulnerable I became. Each story and memory stirred deep emotions within me. At the same time, I felt excited and incredibly motivated, making me eager to jump out of bed each morning to dive into the next instalment.

One of my friends once said, "Writing a book is like giving birth. First, there's the seed. Slowly, it develops and grows into something you nurture and care for, until one day, you're ready to share it with the world." It's a labour of love in every sense, something to be proud of, to love and cherish forever.

Getting it out there, however, can be emotional and exhausting – but also very rewarding. Now, I can truly understand why. I have loved every second of the writing process, even though it completely consumed me. I sacrificed my social life, endured many sleepless nights and found myself dreaming in chapters. Inspiration would strike at the most unexpected moments, often waking me in the middle of the night to record voice notes as ideas flooded my mind. I felt completely frazzled at times, working well into the early hours, piecing together what felt like an intricate jigsaw puzzle. But through it all, I remained committed.

This has been more than fulfilling a dream. It has brought me a deep sense of calm and inner peace. But more than anything, my hope is that these words find those who need to hear them the most, offering guidance, comfort and gentle encouragement to reclaim the parts of themselves they may have lost along the way. If this book can help just one person feel understood and empowered, then every sacrifice has been worth it.

When you refuse to give up, push through your doubts and fears, trust the process and keep going, one day, you'll wake up living the dream you once thought impossible.

If you have a vision, make it your reality. Life may have conditioned you to think small, to stay under the radar, but the truth is, you have unbounded potential, far more than you give yourself credit for. Expand your mind. Break through the constraints of your comfort zone. Push the boundaries. Step beyond what's familiar and make the unfamiliar feel like home. Because the only limits that exist are the ones you choose to accept.

Now ask yourself, if you committed to taking action every single day towards your dream, where do you think you'd be in a year? A step closer or a world apart from where you are now? The choice is yours.

If there's anything that writing this book has taught me, it's that life is what you make it – but before you get to paint the picture, you first have to realise you hold the brush.

Contents

Introduction

I once lacked self-belief in so many areas, but there was always one thing I knew deep within me: I had a story to tell. In that, I trusted my voice, and now that story has become a source of strength, lighting the way for everything I am building today.

Welcome to a journey of rediscovery and renewal, one that has the power to transform the way you see yourself and your life. I am so excited to share this with you, to inspire, uplift and walk alongside you as you prepare to step into the fullest, most authentic version of yourself.

Perhaps you're reading this because, like me, you've experienced times when life feels like a crazy uphill battle. Perhaps you've questioned your worth, doubted your ability to find happiness or wondered if you were destined to settle for less than you wished for. I want you to know you're not alone.

As women, we often shoulder the burden of silent struggles, believing we're the only ones who feel a deep yearning for connection but don't feel deserving of it. We compare ourselves to others, convinced that everyone else is more successful, desirable or loveable. We regret the choices we've made, crying quietly over unspoken regrets or disappointments and sometimes crave love so intensely that it feels like a wound that never heals.

We think we have to put on a brave face while feeling shattered inside. We give up on dreams because we believe they're out of reach, tell ourselves that we're too late, that we've missed our chance or that nobody could possibly want us as we are. We convince ourselves that loneliness is our destiny and that true love is nothing more than a fantasy. And through it all, we silently wonder:

When will I ever be happy?

This book is an invitation to let go of the doubts, fears and limitations that have kept you feeling stuck and, instead, reconnect with your inner light, beauty and the highest version of yourself. It is my gift to you – a guide to self-love, self-awareness, self-respect, self-confidence and self-worth.

Here's what you can expect:

- Rediscover your worth.

- Fall in love with yourself and life.

- Build unstoppable confidence.

- Find the true essence of your being.

- Eliminate self-doubt.

- Conquer your fears.

- Erase limiting beliefs and negative self-talk.

- Overcome your money blocks.

- Overcome the fear of rejection and failure.

- Plus so much more…

And yes, achieving all of this is possible! By sharing my story and the tools that transformed my life, I hope to empower you to take that first step. You might even find yourself thinking, "I can't believe I was stuck for so long!" or, "Why didn't I realise this before?" Perhaps even, "I wish I'd known this sooner." One thing is for certain: You'll begin to recognise just how far away you've strayed from your true self.

This is more than a collection of my personal stories and experiences; it's a powerful call to action. It's a reminder that we are inherently worthy, whole, valuable, deserving, capable and strong. Within these pages, you will find practical guidance, heartfelt reflections and transformative insights designed to help you in every area of your life. (Please note that some people's names have been changed for confidentiality.)

Who am I, you might be asking? My name is Belinda Coleman. I was once the woman who seemingly had it all – married to a high-profile football player/manager, living in the lap of luxury with the world at my feet. But then, after 19 years, it all fell apart. I found myself alone with four children, facing homelessness, financial ruin and unimaginable hardship. As I share my story with you, you'll come to understand the depth of what I went through, how I clawed my way back and ultimately, how I turned my life around.

But before we go any further, I want to express my heartfelt gratitude for your presence here. It's a privilege to have your support, and I'm honoured to serve and guide you on this journey. My mission is to empower women to lead more fulfilling lives, discover their inner light and fearlessly pursue their dreams.

In the following pages, I'll share the missteps I took along the way and how I transitioned from feeling lost, unhappy and exhausted to discovering my true purpose. My aim is to help you navigate your unique path with confidence and clarity by providing insights that could prevent you from repeating the same mistakes I did.

Initially, I started writing this book for a specific group of women close to my heart: the partners of professional footballers, commonly referred to as "WAGs" (wives and girlfriends). While this term is widely recognised and even used in the title of my book, my intention is not to be disrespectful but to highlight the complexities and challenges these women face. Although very much still in use, I believe the label has become outdated and carries limiting connotations that fail to capture the depth and individuality of the women it represents.

Many have expressed discomfort with the term, noting that it reduces them to a single role, overlooking their achievements, ambitions and also their struggles. Their challenges are rarely acknowledged, often misrepresented and overshadowed by unfair stereotypes.

In reality, behind the headlines and labels are diverse and resilient women. Some are entrepreneurs and trailblazers, successful in their own right, while others are dedicated to supporting their partners in a high-pressure, highly scrutinised world. As someone who has walked in their shoes, I aim to offer guidance, support and a deeper understanding of the realities they face while also reaching beyond this group to anyone navigating similar experiences.

Given my background in the industry, you'll notice a distinct football theme running throughout this book. While these experiences have significantly shaped my journey, the lessons I share are universal and extend far beyond that world.

This book is about resilience, adaptability and empowerment – qualities any woman can embrace regardless of her circumstances. The steps I took to overcome adversity are intended to resonate with anyone who has ever felt misunderstood, unappreciated or underestimated.

This book is for you no matter who you are, where you come from or what challenges you face; there is something for everyone.

At our core, we all share the same fundamental needs: to be seen, heard, valued and loved for who we are, which means we are not too different from one another, no matter our backgrounds. We are all capable of transformation, and if I can turn my life around, then so can you. But it does require that you keep showing up for yourself each and every day.

What you are now holding in your hands is more than just a book. You're holding years of life experience, wisdom, self-inquiry, personal growth and resilience-building that have been nothing short of life-changing. Looking back, I honestly don't know where I'd be now had I not made the decision to walk this path. It has given me my life back, piece by piece, lesson by lesson. It has helped me rebuild from the inside out.

More than that, it has helped me step into the happiest, most liberated version of myself that I've been in years. That is why I wrote it: to share everything I know and everything I have learned because I want the same for you.

But transformation is not solely a personal endeavour, it's a collective journey. As we grow and heal, we begin to see our worth, and we naturally radiate that energy outward. It changes how we show up in our relationships in our careers and in the way we carry ourselves. When we share what we've learned, when we extend that knowledge to others, it creates a ripple effect that reaches far beyond ourselves. Think about it: Every person who has ever inspired you, encouraged you or lifted you in some way quite possibly learned those lessons from someone else.

Growth thrives on shared wisdom so it can continue to create a lasting impact that reaches lives we may never directly encounter. That's how change happens, not in isolation, but through the power of shared knowledge, support and connection. Therefore, I encourage you to share this message and the insights you gain with anyone whom you feel might benefit.

Just imagine a world where every person knew their worth, where they felt accepted, unconditionally loved and valued, where they moved confidently toward their dreams. A world where more people chose healing over holding onto pain, where doubt, insecurity and fear no longer dictated their choices. It would change everything: our well-being, our communities, the way we raise our children, the way we lead and the way we connect with each other.

Be that person.

Be the woman who knows her worth, owns her story and stands unapologetically in her power, loving every single part of who she is, inside and out.

Be the creator of your own life because you can, because you always could and because everything you need has been within you all along.

Say yes to yourself and no to fear of rejection or failure. Choose to embrace your inner peace.

And in doing so, you become the proof – the example of what's possible. Simply by stepping fully into who you were meant to be, you serve as the inspiration for others to rise.

And it starts right here, right now – with you.

I look forward to accompanying you on this transformative path.

See you on the inside.

Love,
Belinda x

Chapter 1
Walking You Home:
The Journey Back to You

"Our mind can be our biggest challenge and obstacle, yet if we manage it skilfully, it can be our biggest ally, helping us to reach new heights of personal development and work performance."
– Neringa Antanaityte

This book is more than just words on a page; it's an invitation to embark on the greatest adventure of all: discovering your inner truth. There is nothing more important, nothing more life-changing, than reconnecting with your authentic self, the part of you that exists beneath fear, doubt and insecurity. The real obstacle between you and everything you want – happiness, abundance, love and peace – is not your circumstances, your past or the opinion of others. It is the disconnection from your true nature. The further away we stray from who we are at our core, the more we feel lost, unfulfilled and out of alignment with life. Finding your way back requires commitment. It calls for self-exploration, mindfulness and the willingness to engage with the tools and strategies presented in these pages. As you shed layers of pretence and limitations, you will begin to see yourself clearly, perhaps even for the first time in years.

Before we begin, it's important to recognise that much of the drama in our lives doesn't come from the outside world – it comes from the stories we tell ourselves. The narratives we create are what become the source of our suffering. But have you ever stopped to ask, where do they come from? The truth is, they started forming long before you even realised it, way back in your childhood, when your mind was an open book, eagerly absorbing everything around you. This is when your programming began, shaping the ideas about who you should be and how you should behave. But what if the person you are today isn't you at all? What if all the beliefs you hold about yourself, your worth, your abilities and even your limitations aren't truths at all, but inherited stories, passed down by the people around you that you've carried into adulthood as if they were facts?

Ultimately, we have no control over how our early beliefs are formed. From a young age, we rely on the guidance and influence of parents, family, teachers, society and the media. We're given a name, a religion, taught a language, told how to dress, what to say and how to behave. We learn what is deemed right or wrong, earning praise for good behaviour and punishment for bad. We naturally accept everything we're told because we lack the experience or perspective to question it.

Without a basis for comparison, the rules, values and beliefs we acquire become our own, even though they actually belong to someone else and are shaped by their experiences from a completely different era. At that age, we have no choice but to conform to these ideas and expectations imposed on us. This process forms the basis of who we think we should be, as opposed to who we truly are.

Negative experiences, such as criticism from parents or teachers, can lead us to internalise these messages, planting seeds of self-doubt and inadequacy. For instance, being repeatedly told, "You will never amount to anything," may instil a belief that you're not good enough. These early encounters contribute to limiting perceptions that dictate how we see ourselves, creating what is known as our ego identity. The ego is inauthentic; it is a false representation of us based on our early programming, resulting in a divide between our real self and a persona we feel we have no choice but to embody.

But here's the real question: If so much of what we believe about ourselves was given to us rather than chosen by us, how much of it is actually true? In short, very little. Most of it is conditioning, not truth.

We are not born with limiting beliefs, doubts, fears or an ego. As babies, we naturally express our needs and emotions by crying, screaming or smiling. We instinctively communicate to get the care, affection and attention we need. This pure ability and innate power to express ourselves and seek affection are intuitive and unfiltered. Eventually, societal expectations gradually erode this connection, and we lose touch with our original magnificence.

Babies love every part of who they are, as they have no understanding of the world around them. They are born with an unbridled sense of self-love and fearlessness, but as life unfolds, all that gets derailed, causing us to forget our inherent worth, beauty and feminine power. The young, innocent version of ourselves, once full of life, enthusiasm and trust, has faded. Reconnecting with these childlike qualities is crucial for rediscovering the hidden soul within, free from the need to pretend, manipulate or lie to get what we want.

Now and then, we catch glimpses of our true selves shining through. Those moments where we feel completely alive, present and at peace. It could be the excitement of a girl's holiday dressed in your favourite outfit, anticipating a fun night out. It could be the bliss of lying on a sun-drenched beach, listening to the soothing rhythm of the waves, the thrilling spark of falling in love or the unconditional warmth of a loving pet. These feelings of joy, love and contentment, represent who you already are – it is the *real* you, and because this is our natural state, it is one we can return to. Recognising that you've already felt and lived these positive emotional states affirms their existence within you. However, the ego convinces us otherwise. It creates a false identity that whispers you're not worthy of this. It has you chasing happiness outside of yourself when, in reality, everything you will ever need, every answer you seek, has been inside you all along.

It's our responsibility to reclaim this essence by peeling away layers of our conditioning and dismantling the limiting beliefs we've absorbed over time. The phrase "walking you home" perfectly describes this process, a path of self-discovery and healing. It's about returning to the most authentic version of ourselves, the part that knows our worth and holds the key to the life we are meant to live.

Isn't it incredible that so much of who you believe yourself to be is merely an identity formed by external influences, programmed by your environment, much like a computer being uploaded with data? And isn't it incredible to realise that we have unconsciously been reacting to our thoughts and egos our whole lives? This has not only shaped us but also our reality – without us even knowing! But the good news? Just like a computer, we can be reprogrammed.

This is where your journey begins. To unravel the complexities of the mind, the patterns that hold us back and what makes us tick, we must start at the very beginning, where those beliefs were first formed. We need to examine why they took hold and how we've carried this false self with us for so long.

Recently, I had a conversation about this with a friend. She asked me, "So if this is the case, what do I need to do to find my true self and return to the person I am meant to be? Great question! My answer was simple: You don't have to find anything, there is nothing missing – you've always been complete. Transformation isn't about becoming someone new. It's the process of unlearning everything that made you forget who you are.

This is your reawakening – a return to your innermost essence. You're not broken. There's nothing to fix. It's about releasing the identity that was never truly yours – shedding the masks, roles and labels formed by societal pressure, conditioning and distorted truths. It's about bringing loving awareness to the parts that forgot their light. And through it all, I want you to remember this simple fact: You are and always have been enough.

Some spiritual teachers say there's nothing to heal because we are already whole by nature. However, when healing is spoken of, it refers to the mind – the layers of thought, disempowering beliefs, ego, fears and doubts that cloud your perception and distort your experience. This perspective highlights an undeniable truth – your authentic self is unblemished and pure, just as it was when you were born. Your purpose is to remember it, to reconnect with it. To rediscover the beauty and brilliance that's always been within you. It's about choosing to live from that space now. And when your heart and soul shine from that higher place, you naturally radiate joy, positivity and love – inviting more of the same into your life.

"You attract who you are being, not what you want. "
– Erika Cramer

You cannot get the outside right until you get the inside right, and that's a fact. When a client recently asked me if I could give her the recipe for happiness, I didn't have to think too hard about it:

- Let go of who you think you are.

- Transcend the ego (drop it).

- Practise self-love.

- Speak to yourself with kindness.

- Cultivate gratitude.

- Shift your energy.

- Observe your thoughts without attaching to them and recognise the false narratives for what they are – false!

- Detach from the drama and stop reacting to everything that disrupts your peace.

    - Change your thoughts and beliefs, and your reality will follow.

- Stay in the present moment and connect with your true nature.

- Trust life, stop forcing and start allowing.

- True happiness isn't something you find or have to look for; it's something you create from within.

It all starts with self-enquiry, which requires a deep honest reflection on your life. It's through this journey of exploration that clarity begins to emerge, revealing where you've been and who you became because of it.

The Journey Back Home

Recalling events from our childhood is a powerful way to understand where our beliefs originate. So many of the thoughts we have about ourselves, our worth, our abilities and what we're capable of stem from experiences from our early years when we were learning how the world worked and where we fit into it. Perhaps being criticised for being too loud led you to believe it's better to be quiet. Or maybe, only being praised for achievements made you equate your worth with success. Even the smallest experiences leave lasting imprints, laying the foundation for the identity we eventually claim as our own.

Back then, we would never have thought of challenging these beliefs, and why would we? We were blissfully unaware they even existed. Yet there they were, quietly shaping how we live, influencing our decisions and impacting how we see ourselves.

If you're wondering why we benefit from exploring our childhood memories, you're not alone. Some of you may hesitate to revisit your past, which I completely understand. The last thing I want is for this process to feel overwhelming and uncomfortable for you, but it doesn't mean dwelling on what once was. The whole purpose of this book is to shine a light on the patterns and beliefs we've unconsciously carried throughout our lives. Only when we uncover their origin can we finally begin to challenge them. Were they ever really true, or were they simply someone else's opinions, reactions or fears projected onto us? Looking back enables us to see them for what they really are: just fictional stories, not facts.

Ultimately, we are doing this work to reconnect with the soul of who we were before life sabotaged us. This is the path we must take to step into the highest, most authentic expression of ourselves. When we come home to that place, we find happiness, peace, joy and love waiting there. I know this to be true because my own journey has shown me that this transformation is real. But trust me, the road to freedom is rarely straightforward; it requires strength, commitment and determination before you can finally say, "I'm home."

Take your time, and think back to your childhood to that young, carefree, innocent version of yourself. That child who didn't worry about appearances, whether their nose was too big or their thighs too fat. Who didn't obsess over achievements, money or the opinions of others. Back then, you were open, curious and free to let your mind wander freely. This is who you need to rediscover, not because you're regressing, but because that child represents your true nature.

When I was growing up, I had no idea the perspectives I held were quietly shaping the story that would define who I was becoming. I was completely unaware that an invisible belief system was influencing my thoughts and decisions. This is what it means to live unconsciously, when the ego takes control, defining your perception of yourself and the world without your awareness. It's like living on autopilot, letting life happen to you, believing you are merely a passenger when in reality, you've been flying the plane all along. The moment you realise you are in control, everything begins to change.

I will share my story first; then, it's your turn to do the same. Reflecting on your past may evoke strong emotions, but it's an essential part of personal growth.

My Story

I was fortunate to have a happy childhood. My dad, a strict disciplinarian and police officer, instilled in me values like respect, responsibility and structure. One of the biggest lessons he taught me was that self-discipline is the foundation for a successful life. My mum, on the other hand, was the heart of our home. She was a kind and generous soul who embodied resilience and strength. She showed me the softer, more compassionate side of life, nurturing my brother and me with endless love.

I was six when my parents bought their first house, a charming little bungalow with a beautiful garden that felt like a dream come true. It had a small pond, several fruit trees and a summerhouse, and I remember being so excited the day we moved in. My dad was a hardworking provider, and although we lived within our means, we still managed to live quite comfortably, though there were no luxuries. Second-hand toys, including my first bike, and hand-me-down clothes, were part of the norm for us – we didn't know any different.

My world was filled with curiosity and excitement. I moved through life with a natural sense of freedom, spending much of my time daydreaming and conjuring up stories full of fun and adventure. My happiness thrived in the embrace of nature, immersed in all its glorious offerings, and you could always find me lost in my world of vivid imagination. Our garden provided a canvas for my creativity, where I transformed our summerhouse into a cosy retreat, furnishing it with discarded furniture from my dad's garage.

I was free-spirited and content in my own company, with my cat Martie as my loyal companion. I found endless entertainment in solitary pursuits and spent hours writing, drawing, painting or indulging in crafts. I had a bit of a quirky side too. I collected woodlice as pets, I caught and named every newt from our pond before gently releasing them back into the water – and that was a regular thing in the summer! I invented an imaginary sister, Debbie, who kept me company on the walk home from school. But despite some unusual traits, I was happy in what others fondly referred to as "Belinda's world." And still do, for that matter!

This memory reminds me of who I am at my core: free from limitations, self-doubt, and a fear of judgement, rejection and failure. We all need to return to this version of ourselves: the young, carefree child who believed in infinite possibilities and had the freedom to be their truest selves.

Looking back on those days of simplicity, it's clear how much they shaped my sense of wonder and self-expression. I still remember the joy and freedom I felt in those moments before life's expectations began to pull me away. As I grew older, the innocence and fearlessness of childhood slowly gave way to the pressures and complexities of growing up, especially after my parents' divorce. I remember feeling sad and a little lost as the security of our family unit fell apart.

After the divorce, my mum used her settlement to buy us a small house, hoping to give me and my brother a fresh start. But within two years, we had to sell it because she couldn't keep up with the bills and was drowning in debt, which meant that once the house was sold, we had nowhere to live. The thought of being homeless sent my mum into a flat spin, so she turned to the local council for help. They offered us two rooms in a halfway house, a transitional living facility for ex-offenders, homeless people or those recovering from addiction or mental health challenges.

This prospect made my mum incredibly anxious. I still remember hearing her voice falter on the phone as she begged the council to find us something more suitable. Time was running out, but she reassured us that something better would turn up. Just in the nick of time, days before we were due to move out of our house, we were offered a three-bedroom flat on a local council estate. It was our saving Grace!

Moving to the estate was like stepping into the set of a gritty drama. Unruly characters loitered in the hallways, sniffing glue from plastic bags. Fights regularly erupted on the green behind the flats, drawing residents to their balconies for a front-row view. One incident that has stayed with me was finding a couple in the stairwell having sex. I had to step over them to get to our front door! The constant commotion made me feel uneasy at times, but there was something strangely fascinating about observing this raw slice of life. We were very grateful to have a roof over our heads, so gradually, we adapted to the estate's unique rhythms, finding a sense of community amidst the chaos. I made lifelong friends from there, who affectionately dubbed me the "posh girl" of the estate.

Back then, coming from a "broken home" carried a stigma. Some judged you harshly; we were seen as different, even inferior. I still recall my friend's mum refusing to let me stay over because she thought I was a "ruffian" and a "bad influence" on her daughter. Her judgement had little to do with who I was as a person. It was because I lived with my single mum and we lived on a council estate, and society often viewed that through a narrow, unforgiving lens.

As we settled into this new way of life, my dad drifted out of the picture. By the time I was 15, he had remarried and moved away, and although I saw him a few times afterwards, we eventually lost contact altogether. I couldn't understand why he didn't want to see me anymore or what I'd done wrong to warrant his actions towards me, but more than that, I missed him terribly.

Unknowingly, I carried the weight of his absence, convinced that his departure reflected my worth. Each birthday and Christmas without him chipped away at my sense of self, wondering why I wasn't enough to hold onto. Meanwhile, my mum was doing all she could to keep us afloat, juggling two jobs while trying to keep a tight grip on what I was doing, where I was going and who I was seeing. With tensions often rising between us, our relationship became strained. Her love, though relentless, was overshadowed by the stress of raising two children alone.

The tighter her grip, the more determined I became to break free, not just as an act of rebellion against my circumstances but out of a desperate need to escape the restrictions and constraints that seemed to define my life. I became a "latchkey kid," coming home to an empty flat each day while my mum was at work. By this time, I had two jobs myself, one after school and one on weekends. It gave me some form of independence and a little more control over my life.

In those days, society loved to box us in. We were told, "Be a good girl and do as you're told." It was imprinted on our brains like a mental sticky note. The rules were simple: Settle down and start a family or get a job, and it didn't matter if that job sucked the life out of you. Dreams had to be tucked away, hidden from sight, because a woman's place was in the home, and conformity was the name of the game. I can't remember one person telling us to follow our dreams. Those who did break the mould were rare.

But I wasn't having any of it. I refused to accept the rules society had so neatly handed me. These unspoken expectations dictated what a woman should or shouldn't do, how she should behave and what she could or couldn't achieve. Women weren't meant to challenge the status quo or dream beyond what was deemed acceptable. I was determined to rise above these limitations and create a life on my terms.

Now, as I look back, I see my mum's struggles more clearly. Her love, sometimes masked by the challenges she faced, revealed a fierce determination to protect us. Beneath her frustration, anger and sadness was a woman fighting to hold everything together while desperately trying to reclaim a part of herself lost in survival. I now understand that her efforts were born out of a deep need to be seen and appreciated.

Everything changed when she met Mike, my stepdad. He brought her balance, support and stability, reigniting a spark dimmed by years of hardship. For twenty years until her passing, they shared a love that healed and strengthened her. Together, they became the foundation of our family: Mike, with his dependable and steady nature, and Mum, with her generous and caring nature.

My mum had a vibrant spirit and a vivacious personality. Her love, strength and unyielding will are why I am where I am today. Her words, "You'll only understand when you have children of your own," now fully resonate with me, and I wish I could tell her, "I get it now." She was my rock and my protector and I will be forever grateful for the lessons she taught me.

Sharing these stories with you isn't just about recounting my experiences. I want to help you uncover the deeper layers of your own life. Your story holds the key to understanding who you are and how the events and challenges you've faced have influenced you. By reflecting on your past, your childhood, relationships and defining moments, you gain greater self-awareness, recognising what has been guiding your choices all along. This understanding is a crucial step in your journey towards healing and transformation.

Today, things are very different. We live in a world full of opportunities to transform our lives and pursue the things we genuinely love. With greater knowledge and resources, we can choose our paths and create meaningful, fulfilling experiences. Transformation often begins as a natural progression sparked by adversity and fuelled by the desire to rise from struggle and hardship. I think back to that young girl living on a council estate surrounded by challenges yet holding onto dreams far bigger than her surroundings. Little did she know that those challenges would one day become her greatest strength, not because she clung to the past but because she rose above it. It's not about carrying the heaviness of what was; it's about letting it guide your resolve without letting it define your future.

At the end of the day, suffering is a form of divine guidance, a vehicle for our transformation. You can't truly know happiness without experiencing sadness. Hardship often reveals the hidden benefits of enduring difficult times. In hindsight, you may realise that what once felt unbearable led you to a better place and set you free, despite the upset it may have caused at the time – whether it was a more suitable partner, job or opportunity. On the other side of pain lies growth and the potential for something greater.

Now Let's Unpick It

The Ego

First things first, *you are not your thoughts*. You are not the labels people give you, the roles you play or the expectations placed on you. Beneath all of that, there's beautiful you. Your true self is separate from the constant stream of thoughts running through your mind. This is where the ego comes in. The ego is like an invisible narrator, shaping the story of your life. It tells you who you should be, what you can't do and why you're not good enough. Even though its job is also to protect you from getting hurt, it does so by keeping you small. The real question is: Who is thinking those thoughts?

The ego is the voice in our head – the thinker. Your true nature is pure awareness, who you are beneath the noise. The two can't exist at the same time because your true essence is love, joy and happiness. The ego is negative, which is why the goal is to weaken the ego's grip by becoming the observer of your thoughts. Instead of letting them control you, you take control back.

The ego feeds off fear and self-doubt, convincing you that you're not enough. The trick is to call it out. The next time you hear the ego judging you, telling you you're not smart enough, not good enough or not worthy, simply say, "Oh, there it goes again. That's my ego talking." That simple act keeps you from falling into victim mode. It's like pressing pause on a boring movie and realising, "Wait, I don't have to watch this." By interrupting your thoughts, you gain the power to transform the emotions they stir and, with curiosity and creativity, change the experience with intention instead of reaction.

And that's where true power begins.

Limiting Beliefs

Our beliefs don't stop forming in childhood. As we journey through life, self-doubt subtly weaves itself into the fabric of our identity. It's quiet and unassuming, but its presence is undeniable. That deceptive whisper of the ego, disguised as fear and doubt, questions our worth, chips away at our confidence and holds us back from our potential. At the core of this dilemma lies our limiting beliefs, the deeply ingrained stories we hold about ourselves, our abilities and what we believe is possible. These beliefs act like silent architects, building the walls of our self-imposed limitations, clipping our wings and prevents us from achieving what we're really capable of.

Beliefs vs Thoughts

Both are incredibly powerful but are two different things. You might think one thing but believe another. For instance, thinking "I'm going to start my own business" might conflict with a belief of "I'm not good enough." The belief will win and dictate your actions – or lack of them. Thoughts are fleeting, like passing clouds. On the other hand, a belief is a thought you've repeated so often that it's ingrained in your subconscious. The brain retains information through constant repetition, so the stronger a thought is repeated – whether empowering or limiting – the stronger it becomes. Eventually, it embeds itself as a belief firmly in your mind until you change or replace it.

Now, let's flip that on its head. If the brain retains information through repetition, what stops us from replacing the old, unhelpful beliefs with new, empowering ones? The answer? Absolutely nothing! Consistently repeating positive affirmations, you can shift your mindset. For instance, if you think, "I'll never be successful," you can consciously replace it with, "I am worthy and capable." Or if "I'm always failing" is your go-to, replace it with, "Every setback is a lesson, and I'm growing stronger every day." Keep at it, place a list of affirmations somewhere you can see them and repeat them every morning. Over time, these new affirmations will reshape your beliefs and transform the stories you tell yourself. More on this in Chapter Four.

Now, let me address the elephant in the room. I had a conversation with a friend some time ago, and I'm guessing if she felt this way, then some of you might, too. After much debate, she said, "That whole 'change your thoughts, you can change your life' thing is such an overrated concept, if not impossible. How can anyone change their thoughts when they never stop? The idea of controlling them seems ridiculous to me."

Let's dive into why this resistance exists and, more importantly, how to overcome it.

To be honest, I completely understood where she was coming from. Changing deeply ingrained thought patterns and beliefs is no easy feat; I can fully vouch for that. First of all, it requires consistent effort. It's certainly not something that happens overnight. Plus, our minds honestly never stop, so I absolutely get it. It takes *a lot* of mindful practice.

So, I asked her, "Do you meditate?" She said no.

"Do you ever practise gratitude, repeat affirmations, journal or engage in any other form of mindfulness at all?" Again, she said no.

The thing is, without consistent conscious effort and without the tools to reinforce what you want to achieve, change becomes almost impossible. Yes, it's frustrating, and yes, it feels hard. But engaging in any of these practises daily gradually reprogrammes the mind. It's impossible not to because that's how our beliefs were formed in the first place. It's like training a muscle: The more you practise, the stronger it gets. The same goes for new, positive thought patterns. They need time and repetition to replace the old ones.

The reality is that no, you can't stop thinking, but that's not the aim here. The aim is to stop identifying yourself with your thoughts. You are not what they tell you; it's the ego talking!

According to research, the average person has approximately 60,000 thoughts per day. But worryingly, 75% of these thoughts are negative, and 95% are repetitive! Imagine the rate of self-sabotage! You can see how this repetition can reinforce unhelpful patterns, making it challenging to break free from negative cycles. It's a huge task we have on our hands, but the key to freedom lies in learning to observe your thoughts without attachment rather than getting lost in them. Detachment here means not allowing yourself to be swayed by the persuasive ego. By stepping back and becoming a witness to your mind, you create space for clarity and presence, enabling you to connect with your true self. In this space, you can recognise when the ego is influencing your mindset and begin to regain control. It's not hard to identify the ego. It is the judge in your head, judging you, your circumstances and everyone around you. It's the negative self-talk and your thoughts when they spiral out of control.

What would you prefer: to be caught in the distractions of the ego mind in a negative thinking-feeling loop, or to be connected to your authentic self? Which option do you believe attracts abundance and well-being?

It's quite a simple rule of thumb: You're either conscious or unconscious, a victim or a victor. If you're stuck in a disempowered state, you are dwelling on negativity, which will only reinforce the ego. Until you get this, it will determine your life experience. Life is full of challenges, and we all face them, some more harshly than others. But staying fixated on them keeps you stuck. It keeps the past alive and drains the energy out of the present. Once you understand this, you can take action and start transforming your life.

When you cultivate the witness within you, everything begins to shift. Stop reacting to the drama in your life, and things will improve. When you change how you think, it transforms the way you feel and act. As you begin to diminish your reactive patterns, your entire reality evolves. Drop the negativity and begin planting seeds of positivity. Choose higher thoughts grounded in love, compassion, kindness, gratitude and peace. Let go of the need to make others wrong, and stop judging, criticising and complaining. Take full responsibility for your life and your outcomes. No one else controls the narrative in your head but you.

If you find yourself stuck in a negative loop, pause and ask yourself these questions:

Is what I'm thinking even true, or is it just a story I've created?

What am I feeling right now, and where is it coming from?

What part of me is speaking to me now – my higher self or ego?

What advice would my higher self give me right now?

What would my life look like if I stopped holding onto this negativity?

What lesson or opportunity might this challenge offer me? What can I learn from it, and how can I reframe it?

Transformation always starts from the inside out. By consciously shifting your mindset and managing your ego, you begin to align with your authentic self. This internal change reshapes your thoughts and actions and influences how others perceive and interact with you. The reality is that feelings are the physical expression of our thoughts, so if you want to change the emotion, change the thought. Commit to this and you'll notice positive changes in your life and relationships.

When your mind is consumed by judgment, negativity, hatred, guilt or anger, lasting freedom remains out of reach. These reactions do not support your truth. Instead, they only sabotage your growth, harming no one but yourself. This is the ego mind at play, mirroring your deepest fears and reflecting your inner state onto your outer world. If you constantly blame others or your circumstances, then negativity will be all you see. It will dominate your mood and it is what you will attract. This is karma in action; it traps you in a victim mentality. Simply put, your internal state influences your external experiences, which you are responsible for.

I'll Be Happy When...

If you operate predominantly from the ego mind as life unfolds, you begin to identify with roles, possessions, status and achievements. You might start to believe that your worth is tied to what you do, what you own, how much you accomplish or even how you look. Consequently, you may feel compelled to prove yourself, not just to the world, but also to yourself. Without some form of material evidence to showcase your value, you may convince yourself that you're falling short.

The ego insists that our value is tied to these external factors. It tells us we need more. More stuff, more success, more validation, more proof. Ultimately, this belief consumes us, driving the narrative that our worth is defined by status and possessions, all of which point to the same misconception: that external things will make us happy, which is *so* misguided. The ego is fully responsible for this, perpetuating these lies and binding us to a narrative that external things equal satisfaction, fulfilment and completeness.

Many of us fall into this pattern. And make no mistake about it, I was as guilty as anyone of this. I remember thinking at one point, "Everything will be okay when we move into the next house." But the truth is, it had nothing to do with the house; it had everything to do with what was going on inside me. And whatever those unresolved issues are, you carry them with you – no matter where you go. Instead of facing them, we search for more, and all this does is postpone happiness. This is known as the "I'll be happy when" syndrome. If you're honest with yourself, think of how often you've waited for that one thing to turn up to make your life feel complete.

Life becomes a waiting game, holding out for the dream job, the bigger house, the shiny new car or the soul mate that will supposedly fix everything. But this is backward thinking. Believing these external achievements will fill the emptiness inside you is an illusion. It's a myth we've all been conditioned to believe. Yes, there might be a honeymoon phase when everything feels perfect, dopamine flows and life seems great. But eventually, reality sets in and the thrill of it all fades. Before long, you're bored and searching for the next shiny new thing, trapped in the never-ending pursuit of fulfilment. You're left wondering, "When will I finally be happy?"

Relying on external achievements or validation for happiness leads to constantly searching for something that exists only on the inside. If you don't nurture that inner sense of fulfilment, no job, house, car or relationship will ever be enough. That nagging sense of "something is missing" will always resurface, no matter how much you achieve or accumulate.

When we tie our happiness to those elusive "someday" moments, we unintentionally undermine our self-worth, sending ourselves the message that we're not enough as we are right now. This mindset creates a sense of incompleteness, leaving us perpetually dissatisfied and dependent on things outside us. This cycle is driven by the ego's hunger for success, achievement and approval. Although, let's be honest, most of us have been on this rollercoaster at some point. But that's okay; it's all part of life's rich tapestry. The thing to learn from this is that we have to stop letting the ego dictate our lives and recognise it for what it is – a storyteller!

Overcoming this mindset requires shifting focus to gratitude, self-acceptance and learning to be happy now rather than waiting for external achievements to do it for you. Once you can drop these ego-based pursuits and reconnect with the real you, you'll discover the ultimate cure for everything. Why? Because underneath the pain, heartache and chaos lies pure love, and it's always been there! All you need is to wake up to your amazingly wonderful, magnificent self and let that be the foundation you build from.

But let me be clear: This is not a one-size-fits-all process, and not everybody finds their epiphany overnight. Life is messy and bloody hard sometimes, so give yourself the grace to heal, let go, rest and breathe. As my late mum Brenda used to say, "Slowly, slowly, catchy monkey."

Everyone is on their own journey. Here's what I know for sure: Stories can be rewritten, and thoughts and beliefs can be changed. We can address the ego, no problem. Simply recognising you have a story at all is enlightenment in itself. It doesn't mean you have to be drowning in yours.

The job you have to do now is to get to know yourself on a deeper level, acknowledge where you are, what you've been through and what happened to you along the way. Then, accept it, learn from it and release it. The past is behind you now. It's gone, and you can't change it.

Understanding what I have shared with you in this chapter is crucial because when we want to achieve, succeed, manifest, change or transform our lives, we must first identify what holds us back, what stands in our way and why we give into the forces of the mind. The good news is that when you change your inner narrative, take charge of your thoughts and address your limiting beliefs, your energy vibrates at a higher frequency.

As a result, you not only feel better, you attract better. It's not about forced positivity or pretending everything's perfect. It's about understanding the extraordinary power of your mind and how we can use it to our advantage.

And if the idea of creating the life you would love seems daunting, trust me – it's closer than you think!

Chapter 2
Loving Yourself Whole: The Transformative Power of Self-Love

"If I could give you a gift today, I would give you the ability to see the beautiful gift of love you already are."
– Nelson Mandela

If you're reading this book, you want more out of life. More success, fulfilment, happiness or even the love you've always dreamed of. You've already taken the first step, recognising that something deeper is calling you forward. That desire is no coincidence. It's your inner voice whispering (or maybe shouting) that there's something more for you. And by picking up this book, you've already said yes to that call. That's why you're here. Whatever "more" looks like for you, you've come to the right place. However, there's one important thing to understand. No matter how big your dreams are or how clear your goals are, everything starts with one foundation:

The relationship you have with yourself.

Self-love isn't just a buzzword or a passing trend; it's the cornerstone of lasting success and happiness. When you learn to truly love yourself, something extraordinary happens. You unlock a deep, unshakable confidence that transforms how you move through the world. You stop looking for approval from others because you already know you are enough. Growing up, I had the love and support of my family, but everything changed when my parents divorced. As I shared in Chapter One, being abandoned by my dad at the age of 15 left a deep emotional scar that shaped so much of who I became. It made me question my worth, distorted my ability to trust and confused my understanding of love. For years, I carried this burden, lost in the belief that I wasn't enough, and that love and pain were somehow intertwined. It took me half a lifetime to untangle those beliefs, to realise I was worthy of love without conditions or hurt.

The story I'm about to tell you is my very own love story. It's a story of rediscovery and truth, where I learned that love in all its forms isn't something you have to earn, chase, buy or search for. True love begins within and has the power to heal all wounds and solve all problems. Self-love isn't found in someone else's approval or a relationship. It's discovered in the quiet moments of accepting yourself and showing yourself the same kindness you show others. It's about letting go of who you think you should be and giving yourself the time to heal, forgive yourself for ever questioning your own worth and fully embrace the person staring back at you in the mirror.

Self-love is an inside job. Yes, I know it's a bit cliché, but it's true!

I've experienced painful lessons, heartache and triumphs, running the full spectrum of emotions only to realise that self-love is the most important love of all. Without it, nothing else makes sense or truly works. It is the glue that holds everything together.

The Fairy Tale and Its Final Chapter

Looking back, I realise how much my younger self spent daydreaming. I was captivated by the idea that fairy tales were real and that one day, I would live out my own Disney love story, complete with my Dashing Prince, promising to fall in love and experience eternal bliss. Ironically, I may have manifested that desire because, in many ways, reality mirrored the essence of those aspirations. But just like in a storybook, it reflected the ups and downs of life, filled with unexpected twists and turns.

My early 20s were an especially happy and memorable time when everything seemed to fall perfectly in place. I landed a job as a gym instructor at the Hilton Hotel at Gatwick and quickly worked my way up to a managerial role within a year. Shortly after, I embarked on a backpacking adventure across the U.S. with a friend. It was an unforgettable, life-changing experience that lasted a glorious six months. When I returned home, I ventured into the world of modelling (see Chapter 7 for the full story) and fell in love with the London scene and the exciting opportunities it offered. However, I was determined to buy a property of my own, which meant I needed a stable income. Modelling, as thrilling as it was, was too unpredictable, but thankfully, my brief stint in the industry allowed me to save a good deposit for my first home. It was my next role managing a health club at a hotel in Croydon, Surrey, that became a turning point.

Life was good. I had a great job and a vibrant social circle, and I achieved a major milestone by buying a flat in Epsom, Surrey. For a young woman in an era where financial independence wasn't widely recognised, it was a significant accomplishment. I was proud of myself for challenging the norm and defying the societal expectations placed on women at that time. Yet life, as life often does, had its own script, and an encounter at the health club would set events in motion that I could never have foreseen.

One day, I received a call from David West, the physiotherapist at Crystal Palace Football Club. He wanted to use our pool for two players recovering from knee injuries. I agreed to let them use the club and looked forward to meeting them. My family, all die-hard Palace fans, was thrilled by this news, especially my brother Michael. To be honest, I wasn't particularly interested in football, but that was all about to change.

Around this time, my friend Paul, a club member, invited me to dinner at his mum's house. It was early December, and my colleague Shelagh and I had spent the day decorating the club with Christmas decorations while festive tunes played in the background. A joyful atmosphere was in the air, and everyone seemed to be in great spirits.

After work, I popped over to Paul's mum's house and was greeted by a glamorous, vivacious woman, Pat, who welcomed me with open arms. Paul announced that the Palace match was "on the box" and asked if I minded watching it. Although football wasn't my thing, I agreed, utterly unaware that watching the game that night would mark the beginning of a brand-new chapter.

As we settled down to watch the match, a handsome young man warming up on the touchline caught my attention. The commentator mentioned he was making his debut against rival club, Chelsea FC. His athletic grace stood out immediately, and I found myself drawn to him, watching intently as he effortlessly wove his way in and out of his opponents. When the match ended, I left for home. He had certainly made an impression on me, but I thought nothing more of it because I assumed that would be the end of it.

Or so I thought!

The following week, David West and the two Palace players, one of whom was John Salako, arrived for their first session at the club. John and I immediately became friends, and we'd sit and chat over coffee after his rehab. One afternoon, he asked if I would like to attend the Palace match that Saturday, and I gratefully accepted.

On match day, John picked me up outside the hotel, and we headed to Selhurst Park, the ground of Crystal Palace. As we approached the stadium, I was stunned by the sea of red and blue shirts – it was incredible. The sight of thousands of supporters just blew my socks off. It felt like we were driving through the scene of a football film. I'd never seen anything quite like it in my life before.

Crystal Palace were playing Manchester United, and the energy was electric, with fans chanting and singing at full volume, which was both overwhelming and exhilarating. To my surprise, I spotted my brother in the crowd and called out to him. He came over, somewhat perplexed that after all these years as a dedicated Palace fan, there I was being driven to the game by one of his heroes. He cordially popped his head through the car window and said to John, "She doesn't even know what shape a football is!" (For the record, I do – it's round!)

The match seemed much longer in person than on TV, and I was relieved when the referee blew the final whistle. After the game, we headed to the player's lounge. As we chatted, I noticed the player I had seen on TV. He seemed much taller in person and was extremely well-groomed. He exuded a quiet confidence, and his dark Mediterranean looks made him impossible to ignore.

Our eyes met, and I smiled. He returned the gesture with a warm smile and a nod. Thrilled by this brief interaction, I left that day replaying the moment in my head, convinced that I had just experienced love at first sight. There was an undeniable connection, and it felt as though fate had orchestrated the whole thing. But I had no idea how we might see each other again.

As luck would have it, I didn't have to wait too long! That week, over coffee, John mentioned that I could ask for match day tickets anytime as a "thank you" for supporting his recovery. I decided to take him up on his offer and, this time, invited my brother Michael along, hoping to fulfil a childhood dream for him. Saturday arrived, and I felt excited and nervous as we headed towards Selhurst Park. Once again, the atmosphere was electric, and I finally understood why people were so passionate about football.

After the game, my brother disappeared as soon as we stepped into the player's lounge, thrilled to meet the team, leaving me standing on my own. He was like a kid in a sweet shop, and I was happy for him. But then I saw *him* again! He was deep in conversation with his guests when he suddenly glanced in my direction. Gathering my courage, I decided to go and introduce myself, but my nerves got the better of me. One part of me was saying *do it!* while the other part of me was shrinking like a violet – a bit like a Devil and Angel scenario. The Devil won.

As I approached him, it was as though he'd been expecting me, and we started chatting immediately, which seemed like the most natural thing in the world. I couldn't help but think that our lives were meant to intertwine. We agreed to meet again, but when he asked for my number, I hesitated. Sensing my reluctance, he asked me if I knew the number of the training ground! My raised eyebrow told him I didn't, so he briefly disappeared and returned with a piece of paper with his number scribbled on it. This moment felt like the start of something extraordinary. As I walked away, I felt this was more than a chance encounter. Little did I know, this was the beginning of a story that would change my life forever.

Ironically, after all that effort, I lost the piece of paper! I'd put it in a "safe place" and promptly forgot where that was. After a fruitless search, I had to admit defeat – a true testament to its secure hiding place!

Christmas day 1991 was spent at my mum and Mike's house, just the three of us. During the traditional cracker pulling, a plastic ring fell out of mine. I slid it onto my wedding finger and jokingly announced my engagement to my future footballer husband. At that point, we hadn't even spoken since our first encounter at Selhurst Park!

A few days after Christmas, I plucked up the courage to call the training ground since I had no other option. Fortunately, my timing was perfect. A gruff but friendly voice answered the phone, and within minutes, he'd tracked down the player I'd met, who just so happened to be walking off the training pitch. After a brief conversation with him, he asked me if I'd like to go for a drink. It's unimaginable to think of calling a Premier League club today and casually asking to speak to a player, but back then, that's exactly what happened.

The moment we met again, something just clicked. He was rather reserved at first and let me do most of the talking, which, to be honest, isn't that difficult! But it soon became obvious we had fallen for each other. We spent nearly every day together except when he was away with the club. It felt like we were living in our own romantic bubble, and I knew our destiny was already unfolding.

Three months into our relationship, during a walk, he casually mentioned wanting to take things to the next level. Half-jokingly, I asked, "Do you mean marriage?" To my surprise, he said yes! Although this came out of the blue, I knew deep down that it was meant to be. I suggested he sleep on it, considering we hadn't known each other long. The next morning, he called, and I asked him if he was serious. His response was a confident, unwavering yes! There wasn't a grand proposal or a formal engagement – it simply happened. We didn't need elaborate gestures or a ring to validate what we already knew; just having each other was enough. We announced our decision to our families, and six months after the day we first met, we were married!

Our wedding day unfolded like a dream. It was a radiant June afternoon with clear blue skies. The vintage car we hired wound through scenic country lanes to a charming little church nestled in the Surrey Hills. Steeped in history, it was adorned with intricate carvings and ornate features. As the sunlight danced off the flowers in my bouquet, I felt a surge of confidence and pure contentment. Guided by my grandad's arm, we walked towards the church, where my nervous husband-to-be waited at the end of the aisle.

The ceremony was conducted lovingly by the vicar, and the church was filled to the brim with family and friends, all buzzing with excitement and anticipation. I still remember the beautiful voice of our friend's daughter, Denise, singing *Ave Maria* during the signing of the register, the sound echoing through this sacred place.

After the ceremony, we stepped out into the sunshine and were greeted by the joyful ringing of the church bells, signalling the union of a newlywed couple and marking the beginning of our new life together. As the photographer captured the beauty and emotion of the day, I stood beside my husband, brimming with happiness. It was the perfect setting for the perfect day. Dressed in my white silk gown, I felt like I'd stepped into my own fairy tale, swept away by a tide of love and optimism. Our future looked bright, and the path ahead seemed full of promise.

In the years that followed, we built a family of our own, welcoming four beautiful children into the world – Sonny, Christy, Faraday and Georgie, all within seven years. Life as a footballer's wife was nothing like I could have imagined when we were first married. It was unique and entirely unlike anything I had known before. Looking back, I can honestly say I entered into holy matrimony with my eyes wide shut!

We began our life together modestly, moving from a two-bedroom rental flat to buying a small house nearby. But as my husband's career skyrocketed, we were thrust into a life of extraordinary wealth and privilege. It was both exhilarating and overwhelming. Suddenly, money was no object. We moved into luxurious homes, drove supercars and enrolled our children into private schools, enjoying all the benefits this lifestyle afforded us. We had it all, anything and everything money could buy. Looking back now, I realise how unprepared we were for the pressures and complexities that came with it all.

Despite the extravagance, we remained grounded, surrounded ourselves with close family and friends, creating memorable social gatherings that brought us more joy than anything. Our family life largely revolved around my husband's career. I took the children to most of the home games when they were babies, and they grew up in that world. I was my husband's biggest supporter, alongside his late father, Paddy. Life in the fast lane was quite thrilling at times, and the children and I have fond memories of those larger-than-life days filled with the grandeur and opulence that came with the job.

But this seemingly idyllic picture was not without its problems. We lived in an era where the press had unfettered access to our lives. Public scrutiny, media attention and the constant female attention my husband attracted began to seep into our marriage. Unfortunately, as it has been reported in the press, my husband was unable to resist temptation, which changed everything for me. What once felt stable began to unravel, turning my world upside down and creating a volatile and desperate situation that consumed me. The thing is, when things were good, it was truly amazing; but when things were bad, it was soul-destroying. As the chaos escalated, so did my inner turmoil, leaving me gripped by self-doubt and fear, with the growing realisation that we might not survive the problems that were unfolding.

For many, the world of professional football appears to be a dazzling fairy tale, a life of wealth, recognition and adoration. But beneath that shiny veneer lies a reality filled with challenges, especially for the partners who stand beside their sporting counterparts. Long periods of separation due to club and international commitments create emotional distance. Frequent relocations bring isolation. Then there's infidelity, a topic widely covered by the media, testing the boundaries of love, loyalty and resilience few anticipate. Even the strongest of relationships can be pushed to their limits. Then, of course, when a player is injured or out of contract, the strain of it all can ripple through the entire family.

The life of a footballer's partner is often romanticised as a privilege, and yes, of course, there are undeniable benefits, I don't dispute that. But the sacrifices and pressures? They're rarely acknowledged. Historically, the wives and girlfriends of professional athletes have been unfairly judged at times and dismissed as living a charmed existence. And for the record, I'm not tarring everyone with the same brush here – let me be clear on that. Not everyone faces the same struggles, but my journey and the experiences of many women I've known in this world reveal a far more complex reality that is far more common than most realise. Navigating a relationship in the public eye demands immense strength, resilience and the ability to weather storms that most people never see.

Throughout the disarray, there was undeniable love between us, a deep magnetic bond that always drew us together. He was funny, charismatic and confident. I admired his natural ability to command a room, effortlessly captivating everyone around him. He had an alluring aura, the kind people were naturally drawn to. He would always make fun of me, and I would give him as good as I got. Our playful banter became a source of entertainment for friends and family, often turning into the highlight of the evening. At our best, our connection felt unshakable. But as time went on and the pressures of life mounted, it became harder to sustain.

Suspicion began to cloud my mind. And trust, the foundation of any relationship, started to crumble. The press seemed to know every detail about us, causing an environment of doubt and uncertainty. Mistrust became a constant undercurrent, tainting even our most intimate moments, leaving me questioning whether I could continue living this way. The public persona – the smiling, capable, resilient Belinda – was just a mask. It hid a multitude of emotions. Behind closed doors were arguments, long silences and an ever-widening emotional gap between us. The love that once pulled us back together now felt increasingly fragile.

I began to feel like I was losing myself. My identity was swallowed by the roles I played – wife, mother, daughter and manager of our hectic lives. Wearing the cape of "superwoman," juggling everyone's needs while trying to keep everyone happy. My husband tried to support me in his own way, but his focus was always divided. He couldn't fully understand the depths of my struggle or the silent battles I fought alone each day. The nights were the hardest; I would often lie awake crying, waiting for him to come home until exhaustion eventually carried me into restless sleep.

Some mornings, the weight of it all felt so heavy that simply getting out of bed was an achievement. But no one ever knew. I prayed the dark cloud would pass, but I just couldn't seem to step out of its shadow. I was too ashamed to admit to anyone that I had fallen into a deep depression, so I hid it from the world, pretending everything was okay. I didn't want to appear weak or reveal I was struggling emotionally; it would feel like I was admitting defeat, and I wasn't ready to surrender – at least, not publicly.

Despite what was going on behind closed doors, I always showed up with a smile. My tears were reserved for private moments, and I did everything I could to maintain the façade, particularly for the sake of the children. But the pressure, the expectations and the weight of it all were closing in on me. I was falling apart and knew I couldn't keep it up forever. It was only a matter of time before everything came crashing down, forcing me to face the truth I had been avoiding.

During this time, I sought the help of a therapist named Vanessa, who became my lifeline. She wasn't just a passive listener – she held me accountable, challenged my thinking and gave me the tough love I needed when I strayed off course. Vanessa helped me realise that I wasn't responsible for someone else's choices. Her words of wisdom kept me grounded when I felt like I was losing it, and I will always be grateful to her for guiding me through those turbulent times, for she steered me through some rather painful encounters and helped me make it through to the other side.

Yet no matter how much support you have, there comes a moment when you realise that you've been running on empty far too long, pretending everything is okay when, in reality, you're barely holding on. For me, that moment came unexpectedly. I was getting ready for our neighbour Elio's

50th birthday celebration – a glamorous "white party" hosted by his wife Julie.

Mum and I had spent hours searching for the perfect dress, and I settled on one that resembled an understated wedding gown. As I slipped into my long white dress that evening, it evoked a flood of memories from our treasured wedding day. Those joyous moments felt like a lifetime ago. Things were very different now. It was New Year's Eve, and it was cold and dark outside. As I gazed at my reflection in the mirror, adorned with all the familiar markers of a bride, tears rolled gently down my cheeks. This night stood in stark contrast to that day's bustling excitement and optimism. Standing alone with my thoughts, I knew it was going to be a long night.

Despite the heaviness in my heart, I spent the evening laughing with friends and dancing the night away, wearing the same familiar mask I had become so accustomed to. No one could see the pain underneath. In fact, I believe that I was the last man standing!

I went home alone in the early hours of the morning. The house was silent, and everyone was in bed. I retreated to the lounge, shut the door firmly behind me and broke down. As I sat there, staring out over the garden, it became painfully clear my marriage was over. I didn't want my children growing up in this environment, thinking this was normal. I wanted to set a healthier example and show what love and respect should really look like. I wouldn't wish this for them and I no longer wanted it for myself. I knew, at that moment, that I was done. I had poured so much of myself into this marriage, and now all that remained was emptiness and despair.

My insecurities had slowly consumed me, and eventually, I found myself spiralling down a dark path to the eating disorder Bulimia, which crept into my life when my self-esteem lay in ruins. I no longer resembled the woman who had walked down the aisle all those years ago. I felt ugly, unseen and unappreciated. In a world where I felt powerless, the need for control became an obsession, and the only thing I thought I could dictate was what I consumed and how I dealt with it. I'd become a hollow shell of the person I once was, drained of any sense of self. The life I fought so hard to hold together slowly dismantled me "piece by piece." And then, amid all this turmoil, something unexpected happened that forced us to set our differences aside. My mum had been battling with excruciating hip pain. After various tests and hospital visits, our worst nightmare was confirmed: It was cancer. Watching her vibrant spirit diminish in the grip of her illness was heartbreaking. Each movement was a struggle, a discomfort we would never know, and I knew we were losing her. My husband was incredibly supportive during this time, standing right by my side as I faced one of the hardest chapters of my life. I thought perhaps this could be a turning point for us.

As Mum's condition worsened, she eventually slipped into a coma. For two nights and two days, I stayed by her side, talking to her and gently stroking her face. Her breathing grew more laboured with each passing hour. I held her hand, knowing these were my final moments with her. I just wanted her to find peace. It hurt my heart to see her like this, clinging to life. In the early hours of the second morning, my dear mum took her last breath. I kissed her cheek and said goodbye. It was the hardest thing I've ever had to do.

My aunt Sylvie, my mum's sister, stayed with me that night as my stepdad Mike couldn't bear to see her slip away. I was so consumed by sadness that I barely remember calling him to deliver the news. My mum's passing changed everything. The world felt darker, emptier and less certain without her, and I felt utterly lost.

Sadly, nothing really changed after my mum passed away. Everything returned to the way it was before, and any hope of reconciliation between me and my husband died. I knew deep down things would never change, and I couldn't fix what was already broken. I was mourning her loss while struggling to cope with the unrelenting pressures of my marriage. Things became unbearable, and emotionally, I was in no state to handle what felt like an endless battle. The weight of grief, combined with the relentless strain of a failing relationship, left me completely overwhelmed and exhausted.

Months later, I decided to end my marriage for good. Upon reflection, I sometimes wonder if the timing was my way of distracting myself from the immense void my mum left behind. However, once my mind was made up, I never looked back. The painful truth was that we never fell out of love; I had simply fallen out of trust, respect and friendship.

When I finally decided to leave, I thought it would mark the beginning of a new chapter: freedom, fresh possibilities and happiness. But I was wrong. After spending half of our lives together, raising four children and sharing so much, we suddenly became strangers, even worse: arch enemies. A friend who had recently divorced her footballer husband warned me, "If you think marrying one of them is difficult, try divorcing one – it's a completely different ball game." No pun intended! But she wasn't wrong.

Divorce transforms what was once a sanctuary of love into a battleground of anguish and turmoil. I had hoped for a peaceful resolution and a united approach to co-parenting, but that was just an illusion, and my hope of any form of goodwill soon disappeared.

I felt powerless and vulnerable, thrust into a nightmare devoid of familiarity or comfort. I never wanted to fight, let alone go to battle. The prospect of amicable negotiation faded with the emergence of legal representation, plunging me into emotional free fall, forced to go up against someone I once adored.

Every step felt like a desperate bid for survival as our lives changed into the haunting echoes of what once was, and I felt like I had been thrown to the wolves.

Now I understand that true love cannot thrive without a foundation of self-love and self-respect, and I often wonder: If the love you have with a partner doesn't provide emotional safety and security, is it truly love at all?

We often convince ourselves that love is enough to overcome anything. But the reality is, it isn't. For me, the deeper truth was that I didn't love myself.

What Is Self-Love?

Self-love is unconditional love and respect for yourself. It is the foundation of everything. Without it, you'll find yourself seeking validation from others, rooted in insecurity, doubt and uncertainty, just as I once did. But when you truly embrace self-love you raise your standards and naturally attract relationships that reflect the same love and respect. Your relationship with yourself is a mirror of your inner world. You would never tolerate being with someone who doesn't value you as much as you value yourself.

When you are riddled with self-doubt, it leads to neediness, self-criticism and constant internal battles. Psychologists have shown that the value we place on ourselves influences the relationships we attract. Understand that it is never anyone else's responsibility to make you happy. There's no such thing as needing someone else to "complete" you because, ultimately, you are already whole.

Self-love empowers you to set healthy boundaries, respect your needs and create space for positive, fulfilling relationships. Embracing your wholeness is not an endpoint; it's a continuous journey of self-discovery, healing and growth.

Until you build a loving relationship with yourself, it will be challenging to mend your relationships with others. If you are struggling in any area of your life, start by examining your relationship with yourself. Most of our problems stem from our inability to love ourselves.

Boundaries

People will treat you the way you allow them to. If you don't set boundaries, let things go or avoid addressing uncomfortable situations, you're permitting them to continue. That's where boundaries come in. They are about drawing a line and saying, "This is okay, but that isn't." They clearly define what you're willing to tolerate and teach others how to treat you respectfully. More importantly, when people know where they stand, it prevents resentment from building within you and you will save yourself a great deal of upset.

Setting boundaries isn't just about knowing where your limits are and keeping them to yourself; you have to communicate them. If you don't express your boundaries, people will unknowingly cross them because they assume everything is okay. They aren't going to understand why you've gone quiet or why you've suddenly distanced yourself.

Effectively expressing boundaries means learning how to communicate your feelings without assigning blame. Instead of pointing fingers or criticising, approach the conversation with compassion. For example, you might say, "You've probably noticed that I've pulled away from you because I wasn't altogether happy with certain things, and I'd like to talk about it with you." Then, be clear about what you mean by using examples of their behaviour. Explain how it made you feel, but always start with "I" – "*I* feel upset because…", "*I* felt pressured by…" Don't begin with "you" – "*You* did this…" or "*You* did that."

Another powerful approach is to ask if something is going on with them. They might be struggling with something in their own life. A simple "Is everything okay with you?" can open the door to deeper understanding. This approach avoids the blame game, removes unnecessary pressure and encourages honest dialogue. Often, you'll find they weren't even aware of how you felt or that they've been dealing with their own challenges. Either way, expressing your boundaries helps others see you're not a pushover and sets the tone for mutual respect, as well as being an act of self-love.

At the end of the day, you can't make someone change, but you can set the standard for how you deserve to be treated by clearly demonstrating what you will and won't accept.

The Importance of Respect and Values in a Relationship

While love is essential, respect is the foundation that upholds trust, communication and understanding. Without respect, trust erodes, conflicts intensify and emotional connections weaken. Disrespect doesn't just harm relationships; it also damages self-esteem, leading to resentment and detachment.

Without these fundamental elements, the relationship will gradually chip away at your confidence, and eventually, the relationship becomes unsustainable. Respect and trust are crucial for harmony, emotional safety and intimacy. Without them, relationships become fragile, and love fades under the stress of unresolved tensions.

Your values – such as loyalty, kindness, empowerment, family or generosity – form the foundation of who you are and what you stand for. There is an undeniable link between your values and self-love. When you live in alignment with your values, you demonstrate self-respect, honour your worth and create a life that reflects your true nature. It builds confidence, cultivates self-compassion and strengthens your belief that you deserve love and respect.

On the other hand, compromising your values creates inner conflict, which diminishes self-esteem. For example, if loyalty is one of your core values, yet you break a friend's trust by sharing a secret they asked you to keep, that act of disloyalty can play on your mind, making you feel bad inside.

Respect can also be lost when values differ, and this can apply not just to partners but to friends, colleagues and family members. Have you ever wondered why you feel an instant connection with some people while others rub you up the wrong way? Or why certain behaviours feel like a personal attack? Likely, it's because you don't share the same values with the other person or people. When someone violates your values, it creates tension, and this misalignment is a common reason relationships fail. This is why the saying "birds of a feather flock together" rings true – because shared values create connection, safety, and trust.

We often tell ourselves that love will conquer all, but the truth is that it rarely does. You can deeply love someone, but without respect and trust, the relationship starts to fall apart. More importantly, if you don't love and respect yourself, it's time to change that. Everything begins with you.

When you begin putting yourself first, you say yes to yourself, even if it displeases others. It is an act of self-love. If someone doesn't like it, that's their problem, not yours. Let them deal with it.

Learning to prioritise myself wasn't easy. It took time and patience to adjust, but it was incredibly liberating once I did. When you truly love who you are and know your worth, you don't worry about other people's opinions. You develop a silent confidence, a kind of immunity to judgement, criticism and opposition. It's a deeply reassuring feeling of certainty, knowing that you have your own back and only allow harmonious relationships into your life because you know you deserve nothing less. It feels freeing to know that you would never tolerate bad behaviour from anyone – not for a single moment.

When you come from a place of self-love, everything changes. You attract people and opportunities that align with your values and respect your worth. Boundaries aren't barriers; they're bridges that lead to healthier, more genuine connections. Say yes to yourself and watch your life transform.

Now, take a moment and ask yourself, "Do I truly love myself?" If the answer is no, then congratulations – you've just identified where your work lies. But don't worry, I've got you covered.

Let me remind you: You are not broken, unworthy or beyond repair. You are not too much or not enough. You are precisely as you are meant to be – complete, whole and worthy, right here, right now. By simply repeating three powerful words – "I love myself" – you remind yourself to be kind, accept who you are and honour every part of you.

The best part? There's no limit to how often you can say it, and it costs you absolutely nothing.

So go ahead, shout it from the rooftops and say it to yourself in quiet moments. Write it on a sticky note and pin it to the notice board. Write it on your mirror and have it as a screen saver and say it the second you open your eyes in the morning:

"I love myself."

Chapter 3
A New Path: Finding Freedom in Failure and Embracing Growth Beyond Rejection

"Rejection is just a signpost on the road to self-discovery."

– Wayne Dyer

I thought that I'd endured the worst of my post-divorce battles, but with the threat of homelessness looming over us, I was wrong. My life was about to spiral into new depths of despair. Selling the marital home marked the beginning of a decade of relentless trials and tribulations. Over the next ten years, we moved eleven times, shuffling between various properties, mainly rentals. On three separate occasions, we were forced to vacate our home for reasons beyond our control. There was always a desperate bid to find somewhere else to live, but somehow, I always managed to pull something out of the bag. Our nomadic way of living and the constant upsizing and downsizing felt like being live pieces in a game of snakes and ladders.

This was probably one of the toughest periods of my life. I was fully immersed in a world of turmoil; it felt like I was sinking into quicksand, unable to pull myself free from the ugliness of it all. It didn't feel like just another chapter; it felt like a never-ending feature film with no end in sight. Without the awareness and the insights I have today, I often wonder if I'd still be engulfed in the distorted layers of hurt, pain and self-pity, stuck in victimhood. But then again, a lot was going on for me back then.

About a year after losing my beautiful mum to cancer and walking away from my 19-year marriage, I found myself facing financial ruin while navigating the agony of a bitter divorce. As you can imagine, it was a rather scary time for me, where I pivoted between sadness and frustration to an unbearable sense of loss and loneliness. I wasn't just mourning the death of my mum; I was grieving the loss of everything familiar: my marriage, my stability, even my identity. Fear and uncertainty consumed me, and my world felt alien. I was flailing around in the dark, desperately wishing and hoping for a miracle.

During this challenging period of my life, I found myself on the ropes. Frustration and anger took over, and in desperation, against everything I believed in, I made the unthinkable decision to sell a story to the press. Not only was my life falling apart, but I was desperate for money. In that moment of weakness, I revealed details about my marriage that should have remained private, a clear reflection of the mental and emotional turmoil I was in.

The choice was driven by despair, and while I would never make that decision now, it stands as a reminder of how far I've come since then. My actions clearly mirrored the pain I was carrying, pain that I have long since released.

Sharing my story with you now, there are aspects I choose to wrap in the cloak of privacy and dignity, not out of a desire to deceive or conceal, but rather to honour the sanctity of my experiences and the respectability of those involved.

I no longer resemble the desperate person I was then. She is gone. There are never any winners in situations like that, and I advise against taking the path I did. The only real victory comes from letting go of past hurts, forgiving what may feel impossible, accepting your reality and moving forward with grace.

This period of my life pushed me to my absolute limits. Misfortune hit me from every angle as I fought to manage the constant unrest. But despite the intensity of it all, my focus remained on providing for my children. I clung to the hope that I could find a way to untangle this mess and restore some form of normalcy to our lives. I refused to let go of the belief that I could rise above this uncertain period of my life and somehow turn it around.

We constantly tried to settle into different places, being pushed from pillar to post, packing and unpacking, struggling to find stability. At this point, we were living in a cramped two-bedroom flat; my three daughters shared one room, I was in the other with our little dog Queenie and my son slept on the sofa in the lounge. I was tirelessly trying to stay on top of the bills, including the hefty payments on my car, while dealing with an overzealous opposing divorce lawyer, all in an effort to hold our lives together.

Amid the chaos, I found unexpected meaning. As strange as it sounds, everything began to make sense in a weird and wonderful way. A deep inner knowing revealed that everything I'd been through and was still facing was teaching me something profoundly meaningful. My mum's legacy had given me the means to survive, and it became clear that the resilience she instilled in me had become my salvation. I felt immense gratitude for the 45 years she'd been in my life and realised the gifts of perseverance, determination, love and strength she imparted to me were the very qualities that carried me through these difficult times. For the first time, I fully understood that growth often comes from the lessons born of hardship. I realised suffering is a blessing in disguise.

I came to understand that everything I was going through wasn't there to hurt me; it was there to teach me. It pushed me to uncover strengths and wisdom I didn't even know I possessed. What had seemed like an insurmountable setback revealed itself as a stepping-stone toward something greater. While I couldn't see exactly what that was, I sensed something positive would emerge from the mayhem. But one thing that did become clear is that it didn't break me as I first feared it would. Instead, it broke me wide open.

Though steeped in sadness, this unforgiving period became the turning point for my emotional breakthrough. The experiences I once found intolerable evolved into my greatest lessons. I've learned that life moulds us through its challenges, and despite all the setbacks, I knew I had to keep pushing forward. This newfound awareness shone through the darkness, revealing that I wasn't stuck at all. I was still growing, rebuilding and discovering, which marked the beginning of the journey back to being the real me.

Seeing my life with fresh clarity freed me from a sense of helplessness. It was as if a gentle force had guided me to this revelation. I wasn't just surviving; I was transforming. My struggles were no longer chains holding me back but a pathway leading me to a wiser, stronger and more grounded version of myself. Despite this insight, I knew the road ahead would be long, and before things got better, they were going to get a whole lot worse.

One day, there was an unexpected knock at the door. Not anticipating any visitors, I crept silently towards it and looked through the spy hole. Two burly men stood outside – it was the bailiffs! My heart pounded as I held my breath and prayed they wouldn't detect my presence. I was frozen to the spot. They knocked again, and I was paralysed with fear. After what felt like an eternity, they turned and walked away. My breath burst out of me like a force of nature as I pressed my face against the cold surface of the door, panicked and feeling ashamed. I felt like a criminal. It was a very unpleasant experience.

Within weeks, my car was repossessed, and to top it all off, an eviction notice arrived in the post. I was unsure of my next steps and where we would end up. Fortunately, I received a small financial boost from my ex-husband, which I could live on for a short time, and I managed to buy a small car for £500, which I shared with my daughter Christy. However, with limited options, my life felt like an unrelenting nightmare. Despite everything, my determination to keep my children safe and secure fuelled my resolve.

My next step was to find somewhere to live, so I visited the local authorities for help, drawing so many similarities to my mum's struggles years ago, thinking how much my life mirrored hers. It was ironic, but I finally understood her plight. I also reached out to some local estate agents, desperately looking for a home within my limited budget and against all odds, we secured a rental just one week before Christmas. Moving day, however, was another test of my resilience.

It was late December, and it was already dark outside by the time the removal van was packed up and ready to go. However, the deposit for the new place hadn't yet cleared, which meant we couldn't move in. I was trying hard not to panic and keep abreast of the situation and had spent the whole day making desperate phone calls, all to no avail. The removal men were growing increasingly disgruntled, which was understandable, and my children were cold and hungry, with no solution in sight. It had become a desperate situation, and time was marching on. It got to 5pm, and everyone was looking at me to do something.

In a last-ditch effort, I sped over to the estate agents and pleaded with them to release the keys. Something about my sheer desperation must have moved them because they handed them over against protocol. Overwhelmed with relief, I hugged the agent and thanked him profusely.

That night, as we settled into our new home surrounded by boxes, we opened a bottle of wine and shared an emotional moment. Exhausted from the day's drama, we felt incredibly relieved and very happy. But more than anything, we were together. It wasn't the ideal start, but it was a fresh one, and I was extremely grateful for that.

As the months passed, I stayed positive, hopeful and focused on rebuilding a new life. I threw myself into exercise, got a part-time job packing boxes for the same removal company I'd used for my move, and life began to improve. One summer evening, while out with friends at a local country pub, I noticed a framed quote above the bar that said:

"When you let go, you create space for better things to enter your life."

The words resonated deeply, as though they were meant for me. Standing there, I realised that my relentless need to control and understand everything only added to my stress. At that moment, I gave myself permission to surrender, silently telling myself, "It's time to let go and breathe." That evening, my friends and I planned a Friday night out – just one of many to come.

Enter "The Friday Night Club," a lively group of friends navigating the unpredictable waters of singlehood with enthusiasm. It was time to channel my inner Carrie Bradshaw!

Friday nights became that one night of the week when we dressed up, let our hair down and stepped out into the night with renewed energy and a sense of adventure. With camaraderie as our anchor, I felt like a teenager all over again, rejuvenated and ready for the possibilities ahead. It was like shedding a layer of skin, stepping into the unknown with a mix of trepidation and excitement. Those evenings became our sanctuary, a time to laugh, dance and rediscover ourselves without the burden of our pasts holding us back. For the first time in a long while, I felt alive and slowly but surely, pieces of my old self began to resurface.

We were a fun-loving crew, recently liberated from broken marriages and the trials of divorce. Uncertain of what lay ahead, we finally felt able to step into life with our newfound freedom. We were four women navigating life together, united by a shared determination to have fun and rediscover joy.

Each week, we took turns driving. When my turn came, my daughter needed our car, so I asked my dad if I could borrow his. When I arrived to pick it up, he said, "Oh, by the way, the back window is missing, but I've fitted a piece of Perspex in its place!" Suffice to say, it had seen better days, with its dents and scratches. But it was functional, and I was grateful to have it.

That Friday, after giving it a good scrub, I got myself ready and headed out to go and pick my friends up. On my way there, the Perspex window suddenly flew off into the night. As the girls got into the car, it started to pour down with rain, and Sue, sitting in the back next to the open window, was getting drenched! Ever resourceful, she ran into her house and reappeared with a thin blanket and some pegs. Impressed by her ingenuity, she pegged the blanket to cover the missing window, shielding herself from the rain. Although how she did it, I don't know – we were all crying laughing! This was one of the many escapades we encountered during this time.

We each faced our own challenges, but humour became our remedy, easing the stress of our struggles and offering a reprieve from the turmoil in our lives. It served as a tonic, helping us detach from our worries and reminding us of the lighter side of life. After all, when you're laughing, you can't be sad. Those nights brought us closer together, transforming difficult times into treasured memories. Even now, stories from that era never fail to make us laugh.

Having a supportive network of friends was invaluable. Those days reminded me of scenes from *Sex and the City*, where true friendship became the guiding force that carried us through. The fun and laughter we shared were priceless, a testament to the power of connection and the importance of finding your "happy place" even in tough times.

Amidst the laughter, however, was a fear I couldn't quite shake off – the fear of rejection. Outwardly, I appeared confident, but inside, I was fragile, still nursing the wounds of my divorce. Rejection was the emotion I dreaded most, preying on my insecurities and keeping me within the confines of my comfort zone.

Divorce stirs emotions like a snow globe in the hands of an over-enthusiastic toddler – chaotic, all consuming and impossible to make sense of at first. For me, rejection was something I tried to avoid at all costs. When it came to relationships, I found myself playing games, pulling away emotionally and keeping people at arms-length, all to protect myself. Ironically, it wasn't the rejection I feared most; it was the thought of it. The stories I kept telling myself, the harsh self-talk, the anxiety it caused. I was my own worst enemy, letting self-doubt take the wheel. And the truth? I was the one causing it!

Before we carry on, I think it's important to recognise that rejection and failure aren't the same. Although they stir up our emotions in a similar way, they serve different purposes.

Rejection is when you don't get something you want, like the job, the relationship or the opportunity you'd been waiting for. It feels personal and often hurts. It's like the proverbial door that shuts in your face. Failure, on the other hand, is when you take action to do something, and it doesn't work out. When you don't pass your driving test, your instructor says, "You failed." The frustration and disappointment set in, not necessarily because of the outcome but because of the time, effort and money you've put in. Both experiences can leave us feeling depleted and vulnerable and questioning our worth. But only if we take it personally.

We've all felt the sting of rejection and feared failure, and I had my fair share of both. However, I've learned that life transforms when you change your perspective. Either you react unconsciously to life's challenges and endure the suffering, or you shift your viewpoint to see your situation differently. This simply means that by changing how you see things, you can transform your experience. This concept has profoundly impacted my life and is one I want to share with you because when I fully understood this, it changed everything.

Some of us have experienced it more than others. I swear that after my divorce, rejection and failure were stamped on my forehead as if they were part of the post-divorce initiation club. It was like, "Hi, my name is Belinda. I'm a failure, and rejection is my middle name!" Or at least that's what it felt like!

It's not something I struggle with anymore because now I understand rejection and failure either teach me something or guide me somewhere better. I always learn something from each experience, accept it and move on. If I'd stayed stuck in the "why me" and the "what ifs" and didn't change my mindset, I'd never have accomplished the things I have today, and you wouldn't be reading this book. I'd still be thinking "What if people don't like it? What if it flops? What if I get judged?" You know what I say to that? This book won't be for everyone, and that's okay, but I know it will help someone, and that makes it worth it. Win or lose, I dared to do something different with my life, take the leap and give it my all. And as for the opinions of others? Let them judge. I'm good with that.

My biggest breakthrough came during a period when I was juggling countless responsibilities – a part-time job, school runs, family commitments and the ongoing battle to make ends meet. Despite how much I did, I couldn't shake the nagging feeling that I still wasn't measuring up to expectations. So, when my old neighbour, Maria, offered me the chance to earn some extra money, I jumped at the chance.

Driving through the grand, ornate wrought-iron gates into tranquil parkland, towards Maria's beautiful country manor house and the converted "Old Stables," triggered a flood of bittersweet emotions. The Old Stables had once been our family home. Familiar scenes from my past came rushing back to me. I could almost hear the echoes of my children's laughter as they played in the courtyard, a place that once symbolised freedom, joy and safety.

Maria greeted me warmly, and after a brief catch-up, she took me next door. It was surreal to see the property again, which had since been extended and was now up for sale. Maria and her then-husband Nigel had purchased it from us some years before, and here I was, tasked with cleaning it. How ironic. This house, once filled with family memories, now represented how much life had changed. Yet, as I stood there, I couldn't help but reflect on life back then.

As I worked alone with my thoughts, I felt quite emotional. I couldn't quite pinpoint whether it was nostalgia or a longing for the family unit I once had. As I processed these feelings, I realised I'd been harbouring a sense of failure for a long time. I was convinced I had failed at life, marriage and providing my children with a stable home. I felt like I had failed at being enough.

I eventually sat down for a coffee break, overcome by the thoughts swirling around in my mind. Perhaps it was the irony of the situation, but then, out of nowhere, thoughts of my nan popped into my head, grounding me instantly. My nan had been a cleaner all her life, even taking in other people's washing, which she did by hand using a mangle. For those that don't know, a mangle was a piece of equipment with a handle that turned two wooden rollers, used to wring water out of wet laundry before washing machines existed. On top of that, she had four children of her own, and with my grandad working nights, her plate was more than full.

Thinking of her was rather sobering. Guilt crept in as I realised that I was having my own pity party when, really, I had no right to do so at all. My nan never complained about her work despite her struggles. She just got on with it. Inspired by her resilience, I immediately felt better and grateful for the opportunity. I remember thinking, "Come on, Belinda, stop feeling sorry for yourself. You're alive; you have a roof over your head and food on the table." With that pep talk and a little guidance from above, I felt considerably better.

The grandeur of the Old Stables, which once felt so significant, suddenly seemed unimportant. It was, after all, just bricks and mortar. What mattered was the memories we'd created there, memories that would stay with me long after the house faded into the past. With a renewed sense of purpose, I picked up my cleaning supplies and got back to work. I realised that this wasn't failure; it was perspective. I'd just got it in my head that everything needed to be perfect, and as I understand, that's an impossible standard. I was no longer that woman chasing an illusion of perfection. I was a mother, a protector and a provider but also a survivor doing what needed to be done for my children, just as my nan had done for hers.

This wasn't sacrifice; it was a wake-up call. The past no longer ruled my present, and as gratitude replaced doubt, the fear of failure dissolved. For the first time in a long while, I felt at peace with myself.

I had once been surrounded by wealth, but I'd been reckless with it, which was on me. Still, deep down, I knew I could survive without it. It was no longer about the money but about resilience, determination and an unyielding will to keep going. My four children became my driving force, and if it meant starting over, then I was ready. I didn't always have financial security to lean on, but I had resourcefulness, grit and a fierce independence that had carried me through life before, and this time would be no different.

Then it got me thinking: What is rejection? And what is the fear of failure? It's certainly not about avoiding setbacks, because that would just be impossible. Standing there that day, looking back on my life, I realised that every obstacle is an invitation to pause, recharge and come back stronger. We grow through our experiences, through pain, heartache and challenges; that's a given. But we must turn those challenges into lessons and those lessons into new possibilities. Life doesn't always unfold flawlessly or predictably, but that doesn't mean we're failing. It's about showing up with what you have and trusting the rest will fall into place. This is what you call growth!

Rejection and failure are necessary parts of life. They are guidance from above, redirecting us to something greater and teaching us resilience and perseverance. When you accept this as the truth, you shift your mindset to empowerment, where you can trust that you manage and accept whatever happens. This creates a more constructive outlook, where there's always an opportunity to gain useful insights from the experience. By reframing your thoughts and letting go of the need for perfection, you break free from fear.

Through self-inquiry, the life-changing tools I now rely on, and naturally, the process of writing this book, I've found myself reflecting on my marriage – something that, inevitably, was bound to happen. My views on life have changed so radically since those days, and I am able to see my past in a new light. This realisation allowed me to understand the role I played in my relationship. I no longer regard my past as a series of failures or rejections but as a collection of valuable lessons that shaped the person I am today.

When Failure and Rejection Lead To a Hard but Necessary Truth

I've discussed the importance of choosing how we respond to challenges and how to intercept and control our thoughts. But what if we are too far gone, lost in a world of pain, engulfed in anguish, tormented by the grip of fear? And control? What control? Where do you go from there?

As you know, during my marriage, I struggled with major trust issues, which I internalised as rejection because that's exactly how it felt. I convinced myself that everything was my fault, that I wasn't hitting the mark. So naturally, I pushed myself harder. I tried to do more and please more, often going above and beyond, believing that if I just put in more effort, things would change. But instead of making things better, my efforts only seemed to lead to greater frustration.

Despite my attempts to fix things, everything I did seemed to go unnoticed, and my needs were completely ignored. Over time, a quiet yet relentless resentment began to simmer beneath the surface because nothing I seemed to do ever worked.

In my hurt and desperate need for some kind of resolution, I didn't always respond in ways that served us or myself. I became consumed by the need to uncover the truth, resorting to unsavoury and covert methods that only pushed us further apart. I would also declare that I didn't love my ex-husband anymore, threaten divorce and insist that I wanted to be on my own. These reactions felt like a way to protect myself and keep him on his toes. Ironically, it worked, and they always seemed to draw him back every time, if only to repeat the same cycle, trapped in this unhealthy dynamic.

The truth is, my actions stemmed from deep feelings of sadness, pain and a longing to be acknowledged, understood and valued. Yet, instead of connection, they only ever led to a monumental dose of self-sabotage.

I could only untangle the complexities of my past and make sense of it all when I stopped living in it and I let go of my old story. But it's through life's trials that we find meaning. Gracefully owning your story and taking responsibility for your actions are essential steps toward inner peace and self-discovery. My experience gave me two incredibly powerful tools for navigating post-divorce wounds: forgiveness and compassion.

Now, I can see that I rarely stopped to consider my ex-husband's struggles and what he might have been facing personally or professionally. My trauma clouded my ability to see beyond my pain. Those unconscious patterns of hurt and reaction became part of the undoing of our relationship. The cracks in our fragile bond deepened, creating toxic dynamics that neither of us deserved.

The saddest thing of all is that it didn't start that way. From the very beginning, I entered the relationship with an open heart, full of love and adoration, believing that it would be returned in equal measure.

In my experience, especially when we're young, we give freely, wanting to make our partners happy. We do everything we can to show up as the best version of ourselves, pouring our love, time and energy into the relationship – unaware that all of our kindness, willingness and generosity can be used against us. We're pushed to limits we never imagined, stretched thin in ways we never agreed to. What starts as love and devotion can so easily be mistaken for weakness, and before we know it, we're emotionally drained, disregarded and taken for granted, left questioning our worth.

But there comes a point when the truth can no longer be ignored. The silent sacrifices, the moments of doubt, the countless times we swallow our pain in case we rock the boat that is already sinking – all just to keep the peace. All of this accumulates, layering over us like an invisible weight. We start to realise that love shouldn't be this hard, or shouldn't feel like a constant battle to prove ourselves. That giving endlessly without being met halfway isn't devotion, it's self-abandonment. And the more we try to hold everything together, the more we begin to lose ourselves in the process and we have no strength or energy left to keep fighting against the tide that's slowly pulling us under.

Eventually, something shifts. The hurt, the disappointment and the years of being beaten down finally find a voice, and we say to ourselves, "No more. " But guess what? Suddenly, we're the crazy ones! We're called difficult, dramatic and ungrateful, while our partner conveniently forgets the choices, actions and neglect that led us to this point. The same love that once made us selfless and giving becomes the fire that fuels our strength and boundaries.

When someone finally reacts after years of being dismissed or mistreated, there's always a reason. Pain and anger don't just appear out of nowhere. And those who stand up for themselves, who refuse to be disrespected any longer, aren't losing themselves; they're reclaiming what's left. Sometimes, hitting the point of no return is exactly what it takes to rise again – stronger, wiser and more resilient than ever.

In the end, the writing was on the wall. The relationship could never truly mend without the tools or awareness to break free from those patterns. I've come to understand this truth, and that's why I feel compelled to share it with you here. When we remain unconscious of our destructive cycles and the damage they cause, mending the relationship becomes almost impossible.

There's a fine line between love and hate, and all the mix of emotions that exist in between can cloud your judgement, and you can end up going round and round in circles. It's like running on a hamster's wheel, pouring energy into the struggle but never moving forward. I'm fully aware of how I became entangled in the psychological "merry dance" that defined our relationship. I was constantly battling, not just with my husband but in my head. Breaking free required stepping off that wheel and confronting the deeper patterns within me, but that didn't come until later.

Sometimes, the only way to truly move forward is to end your relationship for the sake of both parties and to set you free. Often, the most loving choice you can make is to let go, and in doing so, you create space for healing, growth and peace.

The thing to remember is that it's rarely ever entirely one person's fault. I genuinely believe there's good in everyone, even those whose actions have caused us pain. Since then, I've grown so much, and like I mentioned earlier, my view of life has shifted to one of compassion and forgiveness. When we approach things from this mindset, we begin to understand that those who hurt us were likely acting out of their own unresolved issues, deeply ingrained beliefs or using their own defence mechanisms to cope with life. Their actions often reflect their internal battles, which may have nothing to do with us at all.

This reminds us that we should never judge someone until we've walked in their shoes and seen things from their perspective. Coming from a place of love opens our eyes and creates harmony in our lives.

I don't see anyone as inherently bad. Instead, I believe people's actions stem from their level of understanding and the tools available to them at any given moment. Some may not yet have developed the ability to live consciously or navigate life with the same emotional awareness as others, and that's perfectly okay. Recognising this allows us to approach other people with greater understanding, even when their actions have been hurtful. Everyone is on their own journey, learning and evolving at their own pace.

If you've faced anything similar to me, now is the time to stop asking, "What could I have done better?" Instead, reframe it as "I did the best I could at the time with the knowledge and resources I had." Hindsight invariably brings clarity, and yes, things may have turned out differently if I had known then what I know now. But that's the beauty of growth; as the saying suggests, it's a journey, not a destination.

Consciousness isn't something we're born with. It's cultivated over time, an awareness that evolves as we learn, adapt and gain insight. The solution isn't to linger in pain or exhaust yourself by trying to fix what's broken. Sometimes, the only answer might be to simply walk away. Show yourself compassion and use kindness over blame, and let that be your starting point for moving forward.

In the end, it's the lessons learned from the things that don't work, which means we learn from failing. After all, it's ultimately what promotes success.

Failure is a detour sign, steering us toward a better route. It allows us to see where adjustments need to be made. It is not a setback but a helping hand that guides us. As for my old friend rejection – it doesn't mean it's the end of the road. It's a case of when one door shuts, another door opens, which could ultimately lead to a better outcome.

Overcoming the Fear of Rejection and Failure

I designed my BRAVE model to help people through heartbreak and breakups. But it's a universal tool that can be applied to every area of life.

It's important to remember that change doesn't happen overnight. We can spend years, even decades, still mulling over the past because it feels familiar, but once we understand how, we can also turn it around.

Breaking old habits and patterns of behaviour takes practice and patience. It might take a few attempts to get the hang of it, but that's fine. No matter how small, every effort is a step toward rewiring your mindset and creating healthier responses. With time, the B.R.A.V.E. method I've developed can help you confront your fears confidently and build the resilience that allows you to grow through rejection and failure rather than being held back by them.

B.R.A.V.E.

B – Believe in Your Worth

Your worth isn't tied to other people's opinions or external outcomes; it's something you define for yourself. Therefore, what value you place on yourself matters because that is the benchmark for how others treat you. Build self-confidence by focusing on your growth and what you can control. When life knocks you down, make a plan to bounce back.

One of my daughters (I won't say which one) faced a tough breakup, and her response was truly inspiring. She signed up for a half marathon, trained every day, enrolled in a remote degree programme and planned her weekly meals to stay on track. Her actions show us that we all can turn challenges around. So, when life gets tough, don't stay down for long. Dust yourself off, get back on the horse and show the world what you're made of.

R – Reframe the Experience

Rejection and failure are simply feedback. When things don't go as planned, ask yourself, "What can I learn from this?"

Looking back at my relationship with my ex, I remember the fear, doubt and low self-worth I walked around with. But over time, I began to see things differently, including the meaning I assigned to the experience. I realised it takes two to tango. Here's what I learned:

First, own your role. Blaming others might feel satisfying, but it only takes away your power and tethers you to an old story. To break free, you must recognise how your actions contributed to the outcome and take responsibility for them.

Second, look for lessons. Every experience, no matter how painful, offers a chance to learn, grow and do better next time. Taking responsibility and holding yourself accountable doesn't mean taking all the blame. It means freeing yourself from the weight of resentment and giving yourself permission to move forward with a clear conscience.

A – Accept Your Emotions

It's okay to feel disappointment, pain or sadness. What matters is how you process them. Give yourself space to grieve or feel hurt, but don't sit in that negative headspace for too long.

When I say, "Accept your emotions," I don't mean letting them control you or lead you into self-criticism. I mean, allowing yourself to feel without judgment. Without judgment for yourself, the circumstances or other people. Then, decide where your energy is best spent. If you're struggling to process things, ask for help. Don't be afraid to reach out for support, whether a friend, therapist or coach. Even journaling your thoughts can help.

Most importantly, don't take anything personally. Avoid spiralling into negative self-talk and take daily steps towards building yourself back up. Sometimes, life's challenges have nothing to do with you. Don't listen to the opinions of your mind or the opinions of other people. Stay in your lane and hold your head up high.

V – Visualise Success

Picture your future self thriving. Imagine the outcomes you'd like to achieve and the life you want to live. Visualisation isn't just daydreaming; it is a powerful way to vibrate at the same frequency as your goals. A guided manifestation meditation is one of the most effective tools for this. It helps you visualise dreams where you experience the joy and fulfilment of living them in that moment. I visualise quite easily by just using my imagination before I go to sleep, picturing it like a movie running in my head. If you think you can't do this, you *can*. Just close your eyes and think about what you want your future self to look like. It might just take a little practice.

E – Embrace Action

Taking action, even when you're scared, is the key to growth. Make a plan and set tangible goals. Create a detailed plan for getting from A to B and work out your next move.

My daughter's story shows the power of action. It builds resilience, reinforces confidence and helps you focus on things other than feeling sorry for yourself. When challenges arise, remind yourself, "I can handle this, and I'll come out stronger. What do I need to do to beat this?" You can't change past events, but you can control what you do next.

When you follow the steps above, you'll stop taking things to heart because you'll realise that doing so only adds to your suffering. Next time you get a "no" from someone, understand it has more to do with the other person than with you. So, don't waste your time and energy rationalising or over-analysing every situation. Accept it, let it go and move forward.

Success

When you step forward and decide to follow your dreams, it's all about venturing beyond the familiar and choosing something new, forging a new path even when it feels uncertain, even when you have to figure things out on your own. But asking for help is okay – in fact, it's essential. Seek guidance from those who have learned from their mistakes and have the experience to share. You'll move forward far quicker than trying to do it alone. Don't think people succeed because they were born to be successful. It's their determination to rise above their fears and challenges and their drive to achieve their goals that sets those people apart. They stumble, they fall but they get back up, dust themselves off and keep going.

Don't believe for a minute that success is reserved for the naturally talented or the lucky ones. It takes perseverance, courage and a refusal to give in to self-doubt. When things get tough, they push through. When disappointment or failure strikes, they accept it, they don't dwell on it. Maybe you might experience a moment of disappointment or a dent in your ego – but don't give it too much of your time and energy.

Let it go and move on. The universe has a bigger plan for you, so never give up on your dreams.

Wherever your fear comes from, make peace with it. Forgive those who've hurt you and cultivate love and compassion in your heart, not just for yourself but for everyone in your life, including those who came to test you. Recognise that your challenges are not obstructions but necessary experiences that strengthen your resolve and help you discover your purpose. With a positive mindset, you can transform challenges and roadblocks and elicit the lessons they reveal. So, when you embark on your next chapter, take with you not just wisdom but confidence and strength. And remember this:

Every "no" is just one step closer to the "yes" meant for you.

Chapter 4
Aligned Abundance

"Formal education will make you a living;
self-education will make you a fortune."
– Jim Rohn

Nervously, I made my way to the front of the queue, hoping that I had enough money in my account to cover my grocery shopping. Then, the dreaded moment came—my card was declined!

So, there I was, the heat rising in my cheeks, wishing the ground would open and swallow me up. I felt completely embarrassed, and no amount of careful planning or penny-pinching could mask the brutal truth: I was broke! There's nothing quite as mortifying as sliding your card into the machine, only for the transaction to fail while you make some flimsy excuse for it not working. Worse still, having to ask the cashier to put things back as a queue of impatient shoppers silently judge you, their sighs and dagger looks speaking volumes.

At that moment, standing at the checkout, I couldn't ignore the nagging voice telling me that I'd helped create this mess. My financial situation was in bad shape, but I knew I wasn't entirely blameless for the position I was in. Shame and regret gnawed at me as I thought about the money I'd squandered during my marriage – a painful reminder of the choices that ultimately brought me to this place of "scrimping and scraping." My biggest concern, of course, were my children. And as much as I wanted to blame circumstances or past mistakes, I couldn't escape the truth of the fact that I'd played a part in this, and it was up to me to find a way out.

I mean, at one point, we were rolling in money. But now? I was reduced to rummaging through handbags and digging behind sofa cushions, desperately trying to scrape together some spare change. As I stood there at the checkout, feeling humiliated, it hit me like a ton of bricks: I didn't like being in this position. Sure, I'd come to terms with the fact that my actions had led me here, but in that moment, the reality of it suddenly became crystal clear - something needed to change.

The Allure of Wealth

When we first married, we were pretty short on cash since we'd spent most of our money on the wedding and honeymoon. But we were happy, just the two of us, and at that point, anything else felt like a faraway dream.

Then, my ex-husband's career skyrocketed, and everything started to change. Suddenly, money was no object, and with it came extravagance. We poured fortunes into buying houses, home renovations, high-end audio equipment, luxury cars and lavish holidays. It was like a dam had burst, flooding our lives with wealth – yet we had no control over its course. The moment it hit the bank account, it was already earmarked for the next indulgence. Not once did I think it would cause the hardship I later faced, something I never saw coming.

We were simply unprepared to handle the fame and fortune that came our way. Financial management wasn't even on the radar. To be honest, I was so focused on satisfying immediate needs and desires that planning for the future felt irrelevant, especially after witnessing the financial struggles after my parents' divorce.

Spending gave me a thrill, whether it was splurging on big purchases, indulging in small luxuries or treating friends and family. It gave me a temporary high unlike anything I'd ever known, and for the first time in my life, I didn't have to worry about money. The sudden freedom to afford things that had once felt unattainable was both liberating and intoxicating. Expensive shopping trips became a regular occurrence, which proved very addictive, leaving me constantly chasing the next "spending fix."

Looking back, I can see how easy it is to get caught up in a fantasy world when you suddenly go from a simple life to one of opulent luxury. You get swept up in the whirlwind, assuming it will last forever, without the foresight or financial wisdom to navigate such a drastic change. It was a world unlike anything I had ever experienced, where people constantly reminded me how lucky I was. To them, we were the perfect family with the perfect life, but many only witnessed the surface level of success wrapped in material gain. Some people enjoyed being part of our world, all while completely unaware of the emotional turmoil behind the scenes.

That's not to say that there wasn't truth in their perception. We shared some incredible times, and there were occasions when our life felt almost perfect. But the game, the pressure, the money and the attention of being in the spotlight don't always equal success. In fact, they can pave the way for failure if not managed well. In so many ways, it could have been a very different story.

My mum, always practical and protective, understood the risks we were taking with our spending habits. She also knew the emotional toll I was under, trying to cope with life in the fast lane and the problems going on in the marriage. I told her everything, and naturally, she supported me through it all. She often urged me to buy a house outright and save for the future, and how I wished I had listened to her, but of course, I didn't. I was blind to the reality that nothing lasts forever unless you care for it, nurture it or plan for it. While there were times of real connection and happiness, the cracks that formed over time became impossible to ignore, and the consequences of our actions ultimately defined our destiny.

Fame & Fortune

Financial issues are surprisingly common among footballers. However, it's not hard to see why, considering they are thrown into wealth at a young age, often without any financial know-how, so it's not surprising that many struggle to manage their finances effectively. Footballers are swept up in the excitement and newfound freedom that wealth brings, caught in the trap of impulsive spending on luxury items and status symbols that match their image. Couple that with a short career span and the unpredictability of their careers, it can be a recipe for trouble. The problem isn't just the money; it's the lack of preparation for what comes next. When their career finishes or ends abruptly, whether due to injuries or out-of-contract periods, the steady flow of income can come to an abrupt halt. Without a solid plan or financial foundation, finances fall apart, and they cannot sustain the lucrative lifestyle they were accustomed to. It's a bitter pill to swallow, but a reality that many face – and one I've seen up close.

I'm a perfect example of why being conscious and intentional with money is crucial, regardless of how much you earn. I had no real understanding or roadmap for handling our finances wisely. I never thought about budgeting or any form of financial planning, nor did I save – not even for a rainy day.

I wish I had addressed these issues then instead of waiting for it all to spiral out of control, but hindsight is a great thing, and life, as we know it, is one big learning curve. The bottom line is it's not about how much you have, but how you handle it.

I learned that lesson the hard way. After our break-up, I became painfully aware of how little I'd prioritised preparing for the future until it was too late. This forced me to take a hard look at my spending habits and mindset and completely rethink my relationship with money. Yes, there were financial advisers along the way and some investments, but even they couldn't save the situation from the poor decisions made or lack of awareness that sealed our fate.

In the beginning, after everything fell apart, I had to take a good look at myself and ask some hard questions: What led me to squander so much money? Why couldn't I hold onto money, and why didn't I plan for our future? What I discovered in my quest to clean up my act led me to a significant revelation:

Money is more than just a physical object, a means to an end or a tool for transactions – it's a form of energy that responds to the mindset and intentions we bring to it. How we think about and interact with money directly shapes how it flows into and out of our lives. It reflects our values, choices, habits and behaviours, making it a dynamic force tied to our beliefs and actions.

My goal became to build a relationship with money that felt authentic and secure.

I no longer wanted to cringe whenever I looked at my bank statements, dreading what I might find. During my period of hardship, those numbers reflected a mindset rooted in scarcity, guilt and self-doubt. In effect, these emotions bound me to financial problems. Reckless spending and people-pleasing had drained not only my finances but also my energy, creating a constant undercurrent of anxiety. I was the perfect example of how unresolved emotions influence our financial reality. This is why taking control of not only your finances on a practical level but also your mindset is essential.

Money Mindset and Beliefs

My relationship with money was deeply unhealthy. Growing up, it sparked constant tension between my parents, resulting in arguments over bills and expenses. I remember my mum spending hours on the phone with my nan, who lived just five minutes away, and my dad couldn't understand why she didn't just visit her to save on the phone bill. Even after my parents divorced, the fights about money continued, cementing my view of money as a source of negativity and conflict.

To me, money became necessary for survival. I buried my head in the sand when it came to financial matters, avoiding the responsibility of managing it, which made it difficult to make informed decisions. When I bought my flat, my stepdad guided me through every step of the process because I couldn't have done it on my own.

When I met my ex-husband, everything changed. I sold my flat, and by my early 30s, we were on our way to becoming millionaires – a stark contrast to anything I had ever known.

Without any prior understanding of money management, I had a narrow view of finances and was naïve about the consequences of my actions. Retail therapy became my refuge whenever I felt unhappy, and it was also a way to retaliate against my ex-husband in a misguided attempt at justice. In some ways, I felt guilty for having so much money while others around me didn't. If I wasn't spending it, I was giving it away to make myself feel better.

Years later, after losing that financial status, I found myself right back where I started – only this time, with less. When I met my ex-husband, I had my own flat, a nice car and a great job. When I left, I had no property or job, my car was repossessed, I had four children to support and I was struggling financially. Surprisingly, losing everything in a material sense didn't affect me as much as people might think because it's where I felt I belonged. I'd been hardwired to struggle. It was the pattern ingrained in me since my parents' divorce – the territory I knew all too well. On an unconscious level, I had been leading myself back there all along. That's how the laws of the mind work.

Looking back, I can see where I went wrong. I used spending to mask my insecurities and fill emotional voids I didn't fully understand. It was evident that my relationship with money wasn't just about numbers – it was tied to my self-worth, boundaries and the guilt that fuelled self-sabotage. Recognising this was essential for my recovery. It gave me the courage to take responsibility instead of blaming circumstances or others. Although blaming others might have been easier, it would have kept me stuck in the same destructive patterns that got me there in the first place. This gave me the clarity to examine the beliefs and choices that had driven me to financial hardship and, more importantly, to begin to change them. While we can't turn back the clock, we can correct the behaviour that created the mess. By addressing the emotions and uncovering the roots of our financial habits, we can unhook from them and build a healthier, more secure future.

Gratitude

Was I grateful for the money we had? Yes, of course. But I took it for granted, assuming there would always be an endless supply. It was as if I had to get rid of it as quickly as it came in, again, an unconscious effort to align my actions with deeply ingrained negative beliefs. I can now see how much guilt played a massive role in this undoing.

Showing gratitude for money isn't just about saying "thank you" when it shows up. It's about respecting its value, being intentional about how you use it and trusting that there's enough for everyone. Gratitude, when deeply felt and expressed, invites more abundance into your life. One way to cultivate this is by practising gratitude for even the smallest things we receive daily – a kind word, unexpected help, a tiny financial gain or simply for being alive! And when I say practise gratitude, I'm talking about practising all day, every day! When we actively look for things to be grateful for and remain open to receiving, abundance often shows up in surprising ways. The more I learned to respect and appreciate what I had, the more I noticed the flow of blessings – financial and otherwise – starting to return to my life.

For example, I've occasionally stumbled upon money tucked away in an old handbag or the pocket of a pair of jeans. When these "lucky finds" appear, I always take a moment to express gratitude. Even when I see coins on the ground, I pause to appreciate them. These small acts of acknowledgement reinforce the belief that you are deserving and worthy.

By consciously appreciating even the simplest forms of abundance rather than dismissing them, you create a mental shift from scarcity to possibility.

In effect, you're retraining your mind to accept more instead of pushing it away. Daily practises like meditation, affirmations and a gratitude ritual can further support this mindset. Personally, I like to start my day with what I call my "growth hour," a dedicated time to focus on positivity and self-development. It sets the tone beautifully for the rest of the day. When practised consistently, a morning routine can change the outlook of your day. When it comes to abundance, consider using the practices below to create flow and make space for good fortune to find its way to you.

Visualisation

Visualisation and an abundant mindset go hand in hand. By vividly picturing your goals and dreams, you train your mind to believe in their possibility, so you focus on opportunities rather than limitations. If you can think about it, then it can become your reality. Everything starts with just one thought, from the chair you're sitting on to your car and house. When you allow yourself to entertain a possibility, you open the door to making it real. If you constantly think about limitations, you will act in ways that reinforce them. But when you believe in a vision, you naturally move toward it. When you take inspired action and match it to your thoughts, the images you create in your mind break scarcity thinking and motivate you to create your reality.

Affirmations and Mindset

Now feels like the perfect time to introduce you to the principles behind affirmations because many people don't realise there are key rules to making them effective. It's not as simple as reading a list of positive words and expecting magic to happen. As I said in Chapter One, the subconscious mind learns through repetition. When you consistently repeat a statement, it becomes familiar, and the mind begins to accept it as truth. The subconscious doesn't distinguish between fact and fiction; it simply absorbs and accepts what it hears regularly, forming what is known as a neural pathway.

To illustrate this, imagine a farmer driving his tractor through a wheat field. If he takes the same route again and again, eventually, a pathway forms through the field. The same process happens in your brain. When you repeat affirmations, you're creating new neural pathways aligned with the message of the affirmation. Over time, as you repeat and reinforce these affirmations, the pathways strengthen and positive thinking and behaviours become second nature.

People give up on affirmations because they often conflict with their beliefs. For example, you might affirm, "This time next year, I'll be a millionaire." But deep down, you don't believe it because another part of you says, "I'll never be successful. I don't have what it takes." The thing to do is make the affirmation believable. Don't go jumping into a grand statement like the one above. Create a smaller, more realistic affirmation that feels true to you, and repeat it daily. This helps your subconscious become more familiar with it; over time, your mind will start seeking evidence to support that new belief.

The beauty of affirmations is that they can overwrite old, limiting beliefs by introducing new, empowering ones.

For instance, if you've always believed "I'm no good with money," you could replace that with, "I'm worthy of success" – which is also a true statement because you absolutely are. This simple shift can change a belief. But you must be aware that the subconscious mind will try to resist change because the ego will fight it, especially if the affirmation contradicts deeply ingrained beliefs. That's where consistency, combined with visualisation and emotion, helps break through the resistance.

In short, affirmations are like planting seeds in the garden of your mind. With committed care, through repetition, emotion and belief, those seeds grow into the reality you want to create. And the best part? Affirmations can be applied to any area of your life.

Repetition + Belief + Emotion = Success

Here are some strong money beliefs to help you get started – and look, some of them are calls to action, too!

"I manage my money wisely and with confidence."

"I release any fear or doubt around money and welcome abundance."

"I am grateful for all my money and the money on its way to me."

"I am disciplined and focused when it comes to my financial goals."

"My relationship with money is healthy and balanced."

Journaling

Journaling and setting daily intentions can significantly enhance your money mindset, improving your financial well-being. And, for the record, you can do this anytime, anywhere, for anything in your life.

Regular journaling allows you to explore and understand your beliefs about money. By writing down your thoughts, you can identify and challenge any limiting beliefs that may hinder your financial progress. For example, you might note that you've been overspending and are hesitant to look at your bank statements. Upon reflection, you realise this behaviour stems from coping with your emotions after a breakup, indicating that spending is used to fill an emotional void. Writing this down makes it easier to recognise and address underlying issues.

Journaling offers several mental benefits. Organising thoughts on paper helps make complex issues more manageable. This therapeutic process provides a release from the incessant stream of thoughts circulating in your mind. By externalising your thoughts, you can reduce mental clutter and clear your head, which improves focus and makes decision-making easier.

Your Relationship with Money

Take a moment to reflect on your relationship with money. What messages did you absorb growing up? Think about your upbringing – what did your parents teach you, intentionally or not, about money? Did they struggle with it, constantly stress about it or avoid talking about it entirely? These early experiences form the beliefs and attitudes we carry into adulthood without realising it.

Are you avoiding financial planning because it feels overwhelming? Overspending to fill an emotional void? Undercharging in business, questioning your worth or undervaluing your skills? Or maybe you're ignoring debt, hoping somehow it will resolve itself? These patterns don't appear out of nowhere – they stem from deep-rooted money blocks. Perhaps you grew up hearing things like, "Money doesn't grow on trees" or "We can't afford that." Maybe you watched your family constantly struggle, robbing Peter to pay Paul because there was never enough to go around, which is a cycle you unconsciously adopted.

Although these messages seem insignificant, they plant deep-seated beliefs that create financial struggles later in life. Always uncover the underlying cause of these blocks and bring them into the light. Until you do, those destructive patterns will continue to play out, no matter how hard you try to get on top of your finances.

Be Careful What You Wish For!

Words are incredibly powerful. What we say sends instructions to our subconscious mind, though it's not just the words that matter; it's the energy and intention behind them. When your words match a true belief and a positive vibration, they act like magnets, drawing the abundance and opportunities you call into your life.

Your subconscious mind is always listening, absorbing everything you think and say. It doesn't analyse, judge or question whether your thoughts are positive or negative. It simply accepts them as truth. Whether you realise it or not, every thought you dwell on and every word you speak becomes an instruction to your subconscious. If you are constantly telling yourself you are not good enough or not worthy of success, your mind will work to make that belief a reality. Your subconscious aligns with your beliefs, actions, energy and choices because, as far as it's concerned, that's what you want.

The language we use influences our thoughts and experiences. When you say, "I never have any money," you're not just speaking it; you're internalising and manifesting that thought. Subtle differences in language can shape our perceptions and reinforce certain beliefs. To create a more positive financial reality, change your language to align with abundance. For instance, positive affirmations like "I am capable of overcoming any money obstacles that stand in my way" can help reframe your mindset toward financial positivity. In short, by consciously choosing empowering words when discussing money, you can transform your mindset and, consequently, your financial experiences.

For example, instead of saying, "I'm broke," say, "I am grateful for the abundance that surrounds me," or "I am doing my best to improve my financial situation."

"It's far too expensive" to "I'm saving for something more important right now." You're still affirming something truthful, but you're also focusing on your priorities rather than on the cost of the item.

"I always struggle to make ends meet" to "I'm currently focusing on finding better ways to manage my finances." This acknowledges your effort and progress without reinforcing a negative mindset.

It's the same principle when talking to friends. When they ask you to go out, instead of saying, "I don't have enough money," say something like, "Thanks for inviting me! Sorry, this week's not great for me, but let's plan something that works for everyone." This response sets a boundary without talking about your finances. It shows you are interested in staying connected. I know it's hard, but you have to repeat lines like, "I'll have to pass" or "I can't make it this time." If asked why, just say, "Sorry, it doesn't work for me." If they insist you join them and offer to move the date to accommodate you,

you can say, "I would love to join you, but I'm watching my budget. Let's catch up as soon as I get back on my feet." This response is honest and relatable and keeps the door open. And by the way, you don't need to say anything about your finances if you don't want to, because it's okay to just say, "No, thank you"!

Changing your language isn't as complicated as it may seem, but it starts with awareness. The more you consciously choose thoughts and words that uplift and support you, the more your subconscious mind begins to accept these new instructions, creating a reality that reflects them. Your words become the bridge between where you are now and where you want to be. You gain control by intentionally using language that upholds positive financial talk, reprogramming your subconscious mind to work for you rather than against you. In this process, your mind becomes your greatest ally.

Spending with Integrity

Ah, now this was my first port of call, to address my spending habits – although it wasn't difficult to see where I was going wrong. Overspending and impulsive purchases were my biggest downfall. Even after my divorce, I felt the pressure to maintain an image of someone with money when the reality was something quite different.

I felt compelled to uphold that image, spending socially to appear generous, and I felt shame for having frittered so much money away. I didn't want people to think I was stingy or mean because I thought people would judge me. I was clinging to a false identity for some kind of validation, which pointed to deeper issues of low self-worth.

To address it, I wrote down everything I'd been guilty of, and overspending was top of the list. As I sat staring at the paper, I realised I had been getting it so wrong for so long. From that moment on, I committed to change that and promised only to spend money with intention, which was hard for me. This meant making responsible choices that reflected my priorities rather than succumbing to impulse or external pressures. I had to be mindful when making any financial decisions, like asking myself necessary questions like: "Do I really need this, or am I just buying it for the sake of it? Is it tied to an emotional need?" It boils down to setting personal boundaries and having the self-discipline to stick to them.

When you're honest with yourself about what you can afford and respect those limits, it becomes an act of self-respect and financial responsibility. This isn't always easy, especially when society constantly pushes us towards consumerism, convincing us through clever advertising that more will bring happiness or validation. But there's no fulfilment in chasing an image; it just breeds feelings of discontentment in the end. By the way, I'm not talking about restricting yourself; what I'm saying is to spend your time and money on what matters to you and brings you joy while also prioritising your future. Spending with integrity puts you back in the driving seat. It starts by acknowledging past mistakes, which, more than anything, will give you a clear idea of where you went wrong. But what this really is about is taking responsibility and committing to a financial plan for moving forward. How many of you reading this now can say that this is habitual for you? It's okay if it's not because you can start today, right now.

To be perfectly honest, I have to be strict with myself when it comes to spending because I love to buy nice things! Then again, who doesn't?! More than anything, I love to give to others, especially my children. For a long time, I felt guilty for depriving them of the opulent and wealthy lifestyle they were once accustomed to. There were times when I thought I had failed them, unable to provide the material comforts they'd grown up with. Since then, I've reset my priorities. I've let go of the guilt, and now I feel nothing but gratitude for everything and everyone in my life.

The legacy we leave behind is not measured by material wealth, but by the beliefs, values and sense of self-worth we instil in our children. To me, that holds far greater significance than any possession. When our circumstances changed, my children showed remarkable resilience, adapting gracefully from a life of affluence to one of simpler pleasures. They always found something positive in each phase, demonstrating the ability to see beyond material comforts. They are four incredible individuals, and the bond we share is one of the most rewarding outcomes of my journey. Together, we've created wonderful memories, always maintaining the fun factor and friendship we've always had – all things that money just can't buy. The most harmonious relationships stem from love, respect and trust, as well as values such as generosity, gratitude, resourcefulness and kindness. These lessons are far more valuable than any luxury, and I take great comfort in knowing I've equipped them with the tools to navigate life with strength and purpose, even when the road isn't paved with gold.

Giving With Joy

This is also known as paying it forward, something that makes my heart happy. Giving with joy means performing a kind act for someone else without expecting anything in return. This practice creates good karma and sparks a ripple effect of kindness, where one generous act inspires another. Think about how uplifting it feels to receive a thoughtful gesture. Now imagine offering that feeling to someone else, whether it's checking in on a friend, sending a heartfelt card or flowers or buying a hot meal for someone in need. Even the smallest gesture can brighten someone's day while filling your own heart with love and happy vibes. If you're feeling stressed or anxious, one of the best ways to deal with it is to go and do something nice for someone else. Being kind and compassionate, instead of feeling hard done by, is serving not just someone else but also you. It is uplifting to make another person smile. That kind of joy is contagious and an instant mood booster.

Let's Talk About Abundance

What does true abundance mean to you? For me, it's not just about money; it's the feeling that there's more than enough of everything to go around, whether it's joy, love, opportunities or resources. Now let me ask you: How do you feel when you read the following affirmation?

"I am aligned with the energy of wealth and abundance."

Do you feel empowered, like it's 100% your truth, or does the affirmation feel out of reach, like something you can't quite believe? I ask this question because if it feels off, it may be a sign of the money blocks or limiting beliefs you're still holding onto. Most people have them, whether they realise it or not, and if left unresolved, like all other mental blocks we might have, they will quietly sabotage your chances of financial success.

Take me, for example. I used to unconsciously find ways to let money slip through my fingers, for the same reason why lottery winners often lose their fortune. It's not just bad luck. It stems from unresolved money beliefs, poor financial planning and destructive patterns, drawing people back to the familiarity of their comfort zone. Without addressing those beliefs, self-defeating behaviours take over, and people with limiting beliefs will undoubtedly end up right back where they started.

Be Happy for Others' Success

Being genuinely happy for someone else's success is a lovely disposition to have. Instead of feeling secretly resentful or envious, try celebrating wins with them. It might not be your natural go-to response to support someone else's success, especially if you're struggling, but trust me, it shifts everything. When you cheer others on, you open yourself up to the possibility that abundance isn't limited. Rather, it's out there for *all* of us. I get that it's easy to compare yourself with others who seem to be having all the luck and think, "Why not me?" But that mindset only leads to frustration and unhappiness. When you genuinely feel happy for others without judgement or bitterness, you attract that same positive energy into your life.

At the heart of aligned abundance is the belief that the universe has no limits, and neither do you. When you delight in others' success, you unlock a powerful truth in that their abundance doesn't diminish yours. There's plenty of everything and it is not limited to just one person. It's also proof of what's possible! So, cheer louder, celebrate harder and let their wins inspire you to keep going. Your journey is uniquely yours, so trust the process. When your moment arrives, it won't just be about what you've achieved, but who you've become along the way.

Your wealth directly reflects your mindset, habits, actions and words, so if you want to change your financial reality, it starts within. Money flows where energy goes. When you treat money with respect and intention, you shift from scarcity to abundance. If you want financial security, the kind that feels solid and expansive, stop chasing it and start aligning with it. This is something you will learn about in the next chapter.

Abundance isn't something you wait for; it's something you claim. Connect with the universe through love, gratitude and the belief that you are already worthy of receiving.

When you change your energy, the world around you transforms.

And that is the real secret to wealth!

Chapter 5
From Vision to Victory: Harnessing the Power of Manifestation

"Whatever you hold in your mind on a consistent basis is exactly what you will experience in your life."
— Tony Robbins

Most of us, deep down, want to change something about our lives. Yet we seem to retreat to the familiar comfort of inaction and let fear, ego and self-doubt take over. The constant lure of quick fixes from social media and the powerful subliminal pull of clever advertising suck us in with the promise of transformation. But without genuine support or accountability, they offer no real progress. Left to our own devices, it's all too easy to fall back into old habits. I think it's true to say that we've all been there at some point, with thoughts of, "Surely there's more to life than this?" I've certainly been there myself, caught in that turbulent blend of wishing, hoping, waiting and uncertainty.

We all possess immense untapped potential, and it's never too late to unlock it. Anyone can create the life they want through mind mastery and successful manifestation. My fascination with this began years ago when I first discovered the book *The Secret* and the concept of the Law of Attraction. At first, I struggled to make it work, but my curiosity drove me to dig deeper. Through trial and error, I uncovered the missing pieces that made everything click. Now, I can confidently say that success in this area isn't reserved for a select few. It's available to anyone willing to commit to the process.

The biggest mistake people make is focusing on what they want – the dream home, the perfect partner or financial freedom. The key to success is matching the emotional frequency of already having these things. That means feeling happiness, security and fulfilment *now* – before those things even arrive.

Think about it. If you want a loving relationship, it's not just the partner you desire but the feeling of being deeply loved. If you want financial abundance, it's not just about the money but the freedom, ease and security it brings. The real key to manifesting isn't fixating on the 3D "stuff," but cultivating those emotions – love, joy, gratitude, inner peace and happiness – that are independent of external factors. That's where true alignment begins. In short, be happy now and let the universe catch up.

My Manifestation Success Story

At the time, I'd never been successful in this area, but I had a good idea of what to do, and I was resolute about changing my life for the better. Once I had made this decision, I was like a dog with a bone, determined and hungry! What I achieved was what I would honestly deem a miracle. Looking back, I realised that my success didn't come from the pages of a book but from a combination of perseverance, action and belief.

I am no different from anyone else, so if I can manifest big results, so can you.

As you read my story, pay attention to how the advice I shared at the beginning of this chapter played out in real life. Within it lies the secrets to successful manifestation.

Way back then, I had no idea how to escape the overwhelming feelings of anxiety, the constant negative self-talk or the panic attacks that consumed me. The more I fixated on those thoughts, the more they became my reality. And therein lies the problem. When we pour our energy into what we don't want instead of what we do want, we inevitably attract more struggle. There's no real hope when we come from a place of fear, doubt or lack. It simply blocks the flow of the universe.

I was exhausted, unhappy, financially strapped and stuck then, but I think you know that by now! I wanted happiness, security and the stability of a family home, but those things felt entirely out of reach. By focusing on hardship, I unknowingly tied myself to a life I didn't want. You see, what you focus on expands, so therefore, you get more of what you're looking at. So, if you are staring at all of your emotional baggage every day, you'll get more of that turning up on your doorstep, trust me!

Deep down, I knew change was possible. I'd studied neuroscience, the power of the mind and the law of attraction, so I understood the theory. But applying these concepts to my own life? That was a different story. The phrase "change your thoughts, you can change your life" kept appearing, and while I understood it intellectually, I was trapped in a scarcity mindset, tangled in a web of past events. I was wallowing in self-doubt, and my mind was clouded by negativity. Suffice to say, my ego was having a field day. But the point is, I was blocking Providence from reaching me.

I remember this moment clearly, the day everything changed.

I was packing up the house for yet another move to God knows where, mindlessly shoving books in a box. As usual, I became distracted and instead of packing, I started looking through the books – my way of putting things off! I was drawn to one book in particular, and I started flicking through its pages. At the end of the book, in big bold letters, it said:

"Sometimes the universe is just waiting for you to say yes."

I took that as a sign, as if something was telling me, "If you want something different, then *do* something different." It was the kick up the you-know-what that I needed. No more waiting, wanting, drifting and negative self-talk. I placed my trust in something greater than myself and made a conscious decision to do whatever was required to change my path. Because to be quite honest with you, I wasn't even on a path. I was on a slippery slope. From then on, I surrounded myself with positive influences, immersed myself in practices that nourished my soul and focused on reconnecting with my values and dreams. Every move I made was intentional, a step away from negativity and towards freedom from the emotional prison I'd been trapped in.

I started making changes to my daily routine step by step. I began envisioning my ideal life, and although the negative thoughts still crept in, I became more aware of them, catching them before they could take hold. I felt the pull of my ego, which created tension, often making me feel like I was taking one step forward and two steps back. But despite this, I knew I had to keep going and maintain my faith in the process.

I began journaling daily, pouring all my feelings onto paper. Writing became my lifeline, providing a release that helped me clear my mind. I created a plan and listed my vision and goals. I wrote about the house I wanted for myself and the children. Every day, I expressed gratitude while walking my dogs and collecting pine cones, which I lovingly placed on windowsills and shelves around my house. Naturally, they caught the attention of my rather curious daughter. She asked me one day, "Mummy, why are there so many pine cones in the house?" I replied, "They're my gratitude cones, darling!" She looked at me as if to say, "You've lost the plot!"

After a couple of months of this practice, I felt a genuine shift within me, and life seemed a little lighter. I knew things had already begun to change. Each morning, I committed to my routine feeling genuinely excited, wholeheartedly believing that everything I envisioned was coming. Daily meditation became a ritual that grounded me, quietened the mental noise and kept me present. It became my refuge, helping me stay aligned with the life I was creating.

Now, we were on the move again, and my rental contract was coming to an end. By now, I'd become fully immersed in manifesting my new life. I was, as they say, "in the zone." I felt happy and at peace with the world, brimming with hope. I visualised my new house in vivid detail, driving up to it, unloading groceries from the car, turning the key in the front door, making a cup of tea and sitting in my lounge on my sofa. I pictured a beautiful garden and felt the immense joy of finally owning my own home. The warmth and happiness of this vision were real, and I truly believed it would one day materialise.

The real challenge, however, was financing my plan. I was working 12-hour shifts at a call centre, and there wasn't much left at the end of the month. To make matters worse, my former legal team was chasing me for a hefty bill I couldn't afford and found questionable. A good friend of mine urged me to seek legal advice from a reputable lawyer, and with the help of a generous loan from my stepdad Mike, I hired a law firm in London.

My new lawyer resolved the issue with the previous firm, which had been the source of my concerns, and also uncovered a critical opportunity that could improve my financial situation. While I can't share specifics due to legal constraints, if successful, it could bring me one step closer to realising my dream. The future began to look promising, and I felt a glimmer of hope for the first time in a long while.

However, I still faced the daunting task of packing up the house, uncertain of our next move. While clearing out drawers one day, I found an old cheque book. On a whim, I wrote myself a cheque for an amount I believed was achievable from my ongoing legal dispute. I placed it beside my bed and acknowledged it with gratitude daily. Despite nearly running out of money and relying solely on my faith in the universe and the legal system, I remained calm and grounded, convinced that my dream would come true.

The Verdict

The day of reckoning finally came. I was nervous but quietly confident. My entire future hinged on this moment. With just £50 left in my account, I barely had enough to get through the week, let alone fund my dreams. It was a make-or-break moment for me: I had nothing left but faith – raw, unshakable faith. My trust in the universe was all that stood between me and my life crumbling around me again.

Each passing second seemed like an eternity as I waited for some clarity. My entire life hung in the balance, relying on someone else's decision. I had visualised this moment for weeks, believing things would turn out in my favour. And despite the pressure of it all, it never really shook my strong reserve. I just felt an inexplicable calm. Deep down, my intuition told me I had already triumphed. I believed with every fibre of my being that I would win the day, and that belief became my solid foundation in this battle of survival.

Then, everything took a dramatic turn, and it finally felt like the wheels of fortune were spinning in my favour. As the final decision unfolded, I felt a surge of nervous excitement.

The result? It was nothing short of a miracle. I was filled with gratitude and relief, and in that moment, I knew that a higher power had been guiding me all along, clearing the path for the breakthrough I so desperately needed. The obstacles that once felt insurmountable now seemed to dissolve in the face of deep conviction and a positive mindset. The universe had aligned perfectly, rewarding my resilient spirit and my refusal to give up.

Though the dream of owning a home was still on the horizon, this victory was a turning point. It reminded me that when belief is paired with perseverance and action, when you ground yourself in positivity, align your belief with effort and the emotion of already having what you desire, the universe can – and will – move mountains.

Humbled yet empowered, I knew anything was possible when you trust the journey and stay true to your vision. With that, I refocused on the immediate task of packing our belongings, which had become all too familiar over the years. With boxes piling up around me, I prepared for our next move.

A Journey of Love, Letting Go and Awakening

My two youngest daughters, Georgie and Faraday, were heading to New Zealand and Australia, with stops in Bali and the Philippines. With the proceeds from the award I received, I could afford a well-earned holiday and decided to join them in Bali. To my delight, my employer graciously agreed to keep my job open for me upon my return. Christy, my eldest, and her boyfriend Elliot decided to join us for one week, while my stay was planned for an additional two weeks.

The move went smoothly as I transported the boxes to our next stop, which was a two-bedroom flat owned by my close friend Jackie, who kindly allowed us to stay there for as long as we needed. With everything packed and the trip approaching, the excitement was building. About a week before our departure, a friend told me about something that sparked my interest – a Smiling Soul retreat in Bali hosted by International Motivator Brett Shuttleworth. It promised a 12-day experience across four unique destinations on the Island, featuring beautiful resorts, adventure activities and personal growth workshops. As I read through the details, it seemed like this had landed on my lap for a reason and presented me with a unique opportunity to explore the possibility of meaningful change. Coincidentally, the retreat was kicking off in Ubud, the same town where we'd be staying. All I had to do was to extend my return flight by a week.

I secured my place on the 12-day adventure and amended my flight, and everything fell into place as if it were meant to be. During the long flight to Bali, I considered buying a house. However, my job in the call centre wasn't enough to secure the mortgage I would need, so I still had to find a way to raise some extra money to supplement my current deposit. I decided to cross that bridge when I came to it and focus on the adventure that awaited.

I had the most wonderful time with my three daughters and Elliot, and with the financial stress behind me, I was able to relax for the first time in years. It was absolute bliss. Bali felt like paradise, with its stunning scenery and delicious food. The beautiful sandy beaches and gorgeous sunsets brought me a sense of peace and tranquillity – something I hadn't felt in a long time. We were having the time of our lives. As the week drew to a close, it was time for Christy and Elliot to go home. I woke up early to hug them goodbye just as the warm sun was rising.

Later that day, Faraday, Georgie and I packed our cases and headed to our next destination: a delightful spa hotel nestled in the Balinese Hills in Ubud, among luscious greenery and paddy fields. We spent a whole week enjoying everything Ubud had to offer, and it was a wonderful experience. Then, the day came to leave my girls and join the Smiling Soul retreat.

A driver picked me up outside the hotel, and I was whisked away to yet another beautiful spa hotel on the other side of Ubud. Our retreat host, Rupali, warmly greeted me. As each of my companions arrived, I knew I was in for a very special experience. All ten of us were searching for the same thing: transformation and connection.

Brett Shuttleworth didn't appear until later that evening, giving us time to bond. Finally, we were summoned to a hilltop open-air building adorned with carefully placed petals and candles, creating a wonderful, soulful atmosphere. Brett greeted us with a heartfelt welcome as we settled onto floor mats. Being sceptical, I hoped that Brett would prove my decision to attend wasn't misguided.

As the evening unfolded, he most certainly delivered! The experience was extraordinary. It began an inspiring journey, awakening my senses and a deep self-love that had been dormant for decades. I felt alive for the first time in years. This retreat changed everything, altering my worldview and revealing how unresolved issues had hindered me.

The 12 days unfolded like a dream, with Brett delivering his teachings with wisdom and precision as we journeyed around the Island, each lesson building on the last, helping me untangle the chaos in my head. Letting go of the past now seemed possible, and I realised that I could trust and accept myself, but more importantly, love myself. It was here where it all began to unravel and where I found clarity and peace, revealing my true purpose – one I couldn't ignore and which ultimately led me here. It transformed from a small, unassuming start to a beautiful, full expression of love. I felt reborn.

As the retreat came to a close in Canggu, we danced on the rooftop bar and watched the sun go down just before our last dinner together. There was laughter, but also tears – tears of joy for the incredible connections we had made and tears of sadness, knowing we had to say goodbye. The bonds formed in those 12 days felt unbreakable, and friendships for life were forged in this magical place. Bali now holds a piece of my heart, and I will forever cherish my time there.

At the end of this rather emotional evening, I approached Brett, overcome with happiness and gratitude, and said, "Thank you from the bottom of my heart. You've changed my life." He smiled at me and replied, "I didn't change your life. You did."

As I lay in bed that night, reflecting on his words, I realised my journey and transformation were truly my own doing. Yes, Brett had offered many insights, unlocking truths I so desperately needed to hear, and had taught me a new way to be, think and feel. But none of it would have mattered if I wasn't willing to change. The real work was mine, and only I could make it happen. This reminded me of something similar my mum used to say to me when I was growing up: "You make things happen in life."

When I returned home from Bali, I felt this new version of me emerge: I was motivated, inspired and ready to take on the world. As I settled back into life at home, I was determined to hold on to this new mindset. It felt like anything was possible. But one lingering goal remained: the dream of owning a house. Refusing to let this ruin my newfound state of euphoria, I threw myself into a daily practice of intention-setting, visualisation, journaling and gratitude, along with my affirmations and meditation.

Brett had reinforced the life-changing power of a morning routine, which I was accustomed to, and I felt more empowered than ever. My new routine gave me more structure and motivated me beyond measure. It wasn't just about starting the day positively. I wanted to maintain that momentum and protect the energy I had cultivated in Bali. I refused to slip back into old habits or let doubt take root. Instead, I created a vision board and an affirmation board, which were placed at the foot of my bed, so they were the first things I saw when I woke up in the morning.

My vision was clear: a house. My dream was now in reach, not just a distant hope.

The House

Although I couldn't yet buy a house, I remained committed to my daily practices, determined to maintain the energetic high I had brought back from Bali. My long-awaited dream – a home of our own – was never far from my mind. I trusted the universe to deliver and believed that sustaining this positive mindset would manifest my goal. There wasn't a doubt in my mind that it would happen.

Then COVID struck! Despite the uncertainty of the situation, I refused to let it throw me off course. I remained dedicated to my morning routine and listened to motivational podcasts every day while walking to my local park. The glorious weather and the opportunity to focus on my well-being made me feel like I was in my own little bubble. During the pandemic, I pursued my studies and qualified as a motivational coach, building upon the skills I had acquired during the retreat. I meditated every morning, and at night, I was tuning into eight-hour abundance affirmations on a continuous loop, designed to reprogram my subconscious mind while I slept – a very powerful tool for manifesting prosperity. This was a time of substantial personal growth as I deepened my self-awareness and significantly improved my relationship with myself.

One day, as I sat in the park in the warm sun, scribbling away in my journal, my phone rang. It was my son Sonny, who happens to be a football agent. He had some unexpected news. He told me that years ago, during a particularly challenging time in my marriage, my privacy had been violated by a tabloid, and stories had been published about our marital affairs. At the time, I hadn't realised the full impact of this intrusion. The details were unsettling, but with legal guidance, I was able to address the situation, which turned out to be my saving grace. I was compensated for this breach of privacy, and the outcome brought an unexpected monetary award that would enable me to see my dream through to the end.

At this point, I was still working in the call centre, but with renewed hope, I began searching for a house. I took positive steps to secure a mortgage and set a budget to guide me. The crazy thing was I eventually found a house for precisely the same amount I'd written on the cheque to myself a year prior. And I believe this is what you call the Law of Attraction!

My vision came to life as planned, which began with just £50 in my bank account, prompted by a letter from my former legal team. My belief at this point was confirmed. Just as we manifest drama, we can also manifest our dreams. This experience reaffirmed the power of the mind, rock-solid faith and determination. A new chapter was about to begin, with the past firmly behind me. I felt grateful and ready to step into my new life, which, just twelve months before, seemed impossible to even think of.

A good friend accompanied me the day I collected the keys to the house. As I drove up to it, I felt a wave of déjà vu. The house resembled the one I had described in my journal. It was incredible to realise that this vision had now become a reality. At that moment, I honestly believed I had uncovered the secret to successful manifestation. I'd become a magnet for my dreams, and it was clear that the energy and vibration I exuded played a key role in making it all happen.

Which brings me to my next point.

Change Your Energy, Change Your Life

To change your life, you must change your thoughts and energy. Letting other people into your head drains your energy and keeps you stuck in old patterns. Don't expect anything to change if these outside influences control your thoughts and feelings. When you allow other people's opinions, actions or words to dictate your mood, you're handing over your power and giving them control of your life. Think about the last time someone angered you. How long did you spend discussing it with others and letting it consume you? How long did you stay mad and frustrated?

Whenever you react to someone's opinion, you let them affect your thoughts and feelings. And when they're in control of your thoughts and feelings, they're controlling you. This is a huge drain on your energy and keeps you tied to a cycle of reacting instead of moving forward.

According to quantum physics and the law of attraction, everything, including thoughts and emotions, carries its own energy. Think about it: When you're at a lively music festival, the collective excitement lifts everyone's spirits. On the flip side, when someone walks into a room with a heavy negative vibe, you can feel the energy drop instantly. Our emotions play a huge role in our ability to attract what we're trying to call into our lives. Feelings like love, gratitude and joy elevate our energy, while fear, guilt and doubt drain it.

Dr David Hawkins's research on human energy fields supports this, showing that every emotion has a measurable frequency. High-frequency emotions expand our energy, making it easier to attract positive experiences, while low-frequency emotions create resistance and block the flow of abundance.

Your emotional state is the foundation of what you attract into your life. To manifest what you want, it's essential to elevate your vibration by surrounding yourself with people and activities that bring you genuine happiness. The key, as always, is consistency: doing things that make you feel good and staying aligned with empowering thoughts and actions.

From an early age, especially as women, we are conditioned to operate in lower vibrational states, which breeds self-doubt, insecurity and disempowerment. When you allow the outside world to define your worth, you unconsciously operate at these lower frequencies, meaning you will attract low-vibe experiences, making it nearly impossible to reach your desired goals.

The moment you take responsibility for your thoughts and emotions, you initiate an upward shift – first through courage, then acceptance and ultimately love. You then align with the frequency of the reality you want to create, which means that instead of reacting to life, you can become the creator of it.

So, ask yourself: Where do you currently stand on the scale? And more importantly, where do you choose to rise to? Your energy is your power, and in every moment, you have a choice. You can choose to either stay where you are, merely responding to your thoughts and others, allowing the past to dictate your present; or, you can transform your suffering and pain into wisdom, allowing it to guide you as you align with the vibration of the life that is waiting for you. If you can think it, you can create it!

Dr David Hawkins's Scale of Consciousness

Elevated States

700-1000 – Enlightenment (highest consciousness, ultimate truth, self-transcendence)

600 – Peace (profound serenity, spiritual enlightenment)

540 – Joy (inner peace, fulfilment, flow state)

500 – Love (unconditional love, gratitude and inner peace - this is where the Law of Attraction works best)

Higher Vibrational States (Empowerment & Manifestation)

400 – Reason (logic, understanding, expanding awareness)

350 – Acceptance (embracing life, releasing resistance)

310 – Willingness (optimism, readiness to evolve)

250 – Neutrality (acceptance, flexibility, no need to control)

Transitional State (Breaking Free)

200 – Courage (the turning point, taking responsibility, openness to growth). At courage, you begin shifting from reacting to life to consciously shaping it.

Lower Vibrational States (Resistance & Struggle)

175 – Pride (arrogance, ego-driven confidence)

150 – Anger (frustration, resentment, revenge)

125 – Desire (craving, attachment, dissatisfaction)

100 – Fear (anxiety, insecurity, powerlessness)

75 – Grief (loss, sadness)

50 – Apathy (hopelessness, despair)

30 – Guilt (self-blame, seeking punishment)

20 – Shame (lowest energy, associated with humiliation and worthlessness)

The higher your vibrational state, the more effortlessly you align with abundance, clarity and purpose. The goal is to move above 200 (Courage) and continue ascending toward states of love, joy and peace, where transformation becomes natural and sustainable.

As you're probably aware, there's no shortage of information on manifesting or attracting the life you want. I studied it until it was coming out of my ears – all the methods, strategies, different schools of thought, webinars and books. But more importantly, I've *lived* it. I've experienced it, and I know what works.

Eight Steps to Successful Manifesting

1. **Clarify your vision.** Get clear on exactly what you want, ensuring your goal is tangible and realistic.

2. **Write it down.** Journal your vision with an action-based statement like, "I am actively seeking my soulmate." Describe what you want in precise detail and set a respectable time frame. Repeat this statement aloud daily. (Remember that words are powerful.)

3. **Visualise daily.** Picture your goal vividly, especially before sleep or in the morning. Use guided meditations, or listen to music to enhance the experience. Feel gratitude as if it is already yours.

4. **Believe it's happening.** Trust the process. Just like placing an order online, you know it's on the way. Affirm your vision with confidence.

5. **Create a roadmap.** Break your goal into actionable steps to plan your route. To enhance this process, vision boards and journaling can be used.

6. **Detach and embrace the journey.** Don't obsess over the outcome. Detach from all expectations, just like you are detached when you don't know something good is about to happen.

7. **Embody your future self.** Embrace the feelings, habits and actions of someone already living that life. You're creating that reality with every thought and action.

8. **Take action.** This is what turns dreams into reality. The universe will meet you halfway, but first, you must take that step.

The breakthrough only happens when everything – your thoughts, emotions, energy, vibration, words and actions – is completely and utterly in sync. This is often referred to as the "flow state."

Energy Blocks: The Hidden Barriers to Manifestation

The universe responds to your internal world, so if your energy is blocked, manifesting what you want becomes very difficult. That's not to say that what you want can't happen, but this is usually the number one reason people experience slow progress or even negative results. It's not that the universe isn't working in your favour. It's that your own energy is working against you.

Here are some practical tips to help you maintain your energy levels:

1. **Organise your environment.** Your surroundings reflect your state of mind. Organised space promotes clarity and focus, while clutter and chaos drain your energy and create mental fog.

2. **Clear debts and obligations.** If you owe someone something, whether it's an item you borrowed or

money, take steps to return it or start paying it back. Leaving loose ends creates unnecessary mental and emotional stress.

3. **Balance your finances.** Financial imbalance often leads to emotional tension. Review your financial commitments, plan to address them and take action to get things in order. Even small steps toward financial balance can free up significant mental headspace.

4. **Let go of things you don't need.** Declutter your life by selling or donating items you may no longer want. This not only creates physical space but also clears stagnant energy, allowing room for fresh opportunities to flow into your life.

5. **Stay on top of admin!** Do I hear a groan here? Yes, you're singing to the choir! But having to constantly catch up with your "life admin" can block your energy 100%. Set aside dedicated time each week to tackle paperwork, emails or other admin tasks. Procrastination on such tasks creates unnecessary stress. A clear to-do list equals a clearer mind.

Now imagine how you would feel if all the above was handled and you had no energy stealers to worry about. Freedom!

Tips and Pointers for Successful Manifesting

Goal Setting

Setting goals requires clarity, strategy and commitment. Using the S.M.A.R.T framework ensures your goals are specific, measurable, achievable, relevant and time-bound, making them more actionable and attainable. For example, if your goal is to improve your health and fitness, it might look like this:

> "I will exercise for 30 minutes, five days a week, for the next three months to improve my physical fitness and energy levels."

Here you have covered every point:

Specific: Stated exercise frequency and duration.

Measurable: Set the duration to a minimum of 30 minutes, five times a week.

Achievable: The plan is both reasonable and flexible.

Relevant: The goal contributes to better health and energy.

Time-bound: The three-month period ensures accountability.

Remember to make a record of whatever your goal may be; I'm a massive fan of writing things down because it helps to solidify your intentions, keeps you accountable and gives you a tangible reminder of what you're working towards.

Belief

Developing an unshakable belief in what you want to create is a critical step in making your dreams a reality. So, go ahead and dare to dream! That vision is the fuel that lights your passion, but your *belief* is the force that shields you from doubt. Beyond just believing in your dreams, you must also believe in your potential, your strengths and your talents.

Intentional Energy

Manifestation is about being intentional with your energy. It's about creating the right foundation where your thoughts, feelings and actions align with your desires. Think of a time when you felt amazing, your energy was high and everything seemed to flow effortlessly. Now grab your journal and ask yourself:

What was I doing?

Who was I spending time with?

What activities made me feel happy and alive?

What goals or aspirations was I actively pursuing?

Now flip it:

What has changed since then?

Have I stopped doing the things that made me feel good?

Am I surrounding myself with the right people?

Answering these questions can help you see where you've drifted off track and what small changes you can make to return to feeling like your best self. You also might want to consider this exercise when you are generally out of sorts.

Meditation

Meditation is a powerful tool for inner peace, self-awareness and manifestation. It acts as a bridge between your outer world and inner self, allowing you to quiet the mind and focus on the present – the only place where real change happens. Concentrating on your breath and calming mental noise releases past burdens and creates space for clarity, new beliefs and aligned action. In this stillness, you become more receptive to abundance, love and success, transforming your energy to match your dreams.

An Attitude of Gratitude

I know I have already touched on this in Chapter Four, but gratitude is one of the most powerful emotions you can cultivate. It instantly shifts your vibration to a higher frequency, matching it to that of abundance and opening you up to receiving. It's always important to be grateful for what you have and what's coming, so give thanks as if you have already received what you want to attract. This attitude takes you from a state of lack to a state of abundance – and remember: You attract what you are, not what you want. When you are in a state of gratitude, you attract more things for which you are grateful.

Balance

In the world of manifestation, your energy is your currency. When you're out of balance, you lose your power and unintentionally block your ability to attract. It's easy to get caught up in life's drama, where jealousy, anger or resentment drain you and distort your thoughts. The real work is transforming these low-energy emotions into high-energy vibrations. Turn anger into compassion and let jealousy guide you to kindness and resentment into love. Think that's hard? It might be for some, but this is all about changing perspectives! What matters is learning to manage your emotions so that they serve you rather than control you.

Balance isn't optional. It's essential for success. Start addressing the patterns that might be causing an imbalance. Are you caught in the blame game? Unable to sleep because you're replaying your drama from your relationship or job? Seeking validation? All this is doing is feeding the ego.

Instead, strengthen your self-worth by focusing on self-love and compassion.

Pause here and ask yourself, "How can I bring balance to my life by changing my attitude?" Think of your career, relationships, finances or spirituality. Another journal moment here, I think!

Comparison

Never compare yourself to others. Embrace your individuality and let go of the idea that you have to keep up with anyone. Your journey is uniquely yours. Comparison carries envy and resentment. They are toxins that corrode the soul, and the only one you are hurting is you. Drop all that. It doesn't matter what anyone else has got or what they look like! Instead, focus on making your life fantastic. And if people are looking at you through the eyes of envy, that's on them.

Integrity

If you're manifesting from a place of dishonesty, inauthenticity or manipulation, you create resistance. Integrity means being honest about your desires, taking action that aligns with your values and staying true to your word.

So, if your goal is to lose a stone, but all you do is eat takeaways and you fail to turn up to your PT session, then you are breaking your word with the universe and life will let you know about it with subpar results. If you constantly break promises to yourself, make excuses or operate in a way that goes against your values, you subconsciously signal that you don't trust yourself to follow through. It's that energy that blocks your ability to receive.

Your Environment

What you focus on the most dictates your results. Just take a moment to reflect on your circumstances and the people you spend the most time with. It can reveal so much. Unhealthy relationships or negative influences can drain your energy, making it clear that your external environment can pull you down just as much as your internal one.

Surround yourself with uplifting people who inspire and energise you. Avoid those who criticise others, complain, gossip or dwell on negativity, as this will sap your energy and lower your vibe. This creates a frequency that makes manifestation almost impossible.

More importantly, when you don't believe you're deserving, capable or good enough, your dreams effectively get cancelled out.

The beautiful thing about this process is that it's a journey of self-transformation and mind mastery. It's not just about ticking off your wish list; it's actually so much more than people realise. It's a process that helps you shift from chaos to clarity, doubt to belief and resistance to flow. It guides you to confront and heal the parts of you that have been holding you back. It's a transformational bridge between who you are now and who you are capable of becoming: the person who can receive, sustain and thrive in harmony with your goals and aspirations.

Manifestation reveals that the life you dream of isn't waiting for you in some far-off land. It starts as you cultivate the thoughts, beliefs and actions that become the perfect match for your vision.

In your quest to reach your goals, you may find the most unbelievable outcomes, which can change the course of your life – just like it did mine. You know when you've been successful because you recognise that your external reality is a reflection of your inner world.

To wrap this up, I want to address something my daughter said to me while I was writing this. After reading this chapter, she remarked, "Yes but you had opportunities where there was always a possibility of you receiving that money."

Her comment made me pause and reflect because, on the surface, it's true – there were opportunities. But I explained to her that it's not as simple as having opportunities. One of those situations could have completely backfired, and the other might never have materialised if conditions hadn't synchronised perfectly.

This is an important point I want to stress: Opportunities don't guarantee outcomes. Manifestation isn't about expecting everything to fall into place without effort, intention or alignment. You can be presented with the most incredible chance, but if you're not energetically matched with it, and you're coming from a place of doubt or fear or operating from a scarcity mindset, it may elude you.

The "good fortune" I experienced didn't just happen by chance. It required me to be in a place where I was open to receiving it. I had to work on myself, my thoughts, beliefs and actions so that when those opportunities came, I could meet them with the right energy. If I'd been in a negative state or acted out of desperation, the outcome could have been entirely different.

If you're constantly reacting to your environment, then you're letting your surroundings and the people in it dictate your life. But when you stop worrying about what other people think or say and focus on what you think and feel, you'll notice a big difference in your energy levels.

Leave other people's judgement at the door. It's none of your business, and they have nothing to do with who you really are. Stop reacting and start creating. Protect your energy, focus on your path and reclaim your inner peace. When you do this and restore your energy, your life will change.

The lesson here is that while openings may come your way, your ability to align with them and trust the process turns possibility into reality. Without that alignment, the same opportunity could pass you by. So, it's not just about the doors that open – it's about whether you're ready to walk through them.

Chapter 6
A Fragile Line:
Trust, Betrayal and
Everything In-Between

It's not about finding the perfect mate to be happy.
It's about being happy first to attract the right one.

When I finally started rebuilding my life, I realised how low self-worth can shape our decisions, especially in relationships, whether staying in a situation where you feel unseen, settling for less or avoiding love altogether out of fear of being hurt. It generally boils down to how much or how little you value yourself.

I've worked with many women who've struggled with this. Women who've poured everything into their relationships but lost sight of who they are. Some have made do with breadcrumbs, convinced that asking for more would push their partner away, so they play small and put up with unacceptable behaviour. I know women who've built walls so high that they've forgotten what it's like to feel love. Their hearts are either broken or closed, and they feel their chances of finding love are limited.

Take my client, Catherine, for instance. She first came to me because her last boyfriend had cheated on her. Now she was back again, and as I listened to her story, it sounded all too familiar. She constantly threw herself into her relationships, believing she could shape each man into her ideal partner, even when it was clear he was never going to be. Catherine, a striking, well-groomed woman, was head of marketing for a global company and was never short of admirers. Yet, she valued being in a relationship more than being alone, even if it meant being in an unhealthy one, as she was convinced she needed a man to be happy.

When I first met Catherine, I asked her about her family, and it became clear that her need for validation stemmed from her childhood. Catherine endured years of verbal abuse from her stepfather, who cruelly belittled her, while her mother looked the other way, allowing his toxic behaviour to continuously upset her daughter. This neglect left Catherine feeling unloved and deeply resentful.

When Catherine shared this account of what she'd endured during her upbringing, I understood the root of her self-doubt. Her stepfather's mental abuse, combined with her mother's indifference, left her feeling worthless, drawing her to partners who mirrored the same disregard and the same toxic patterns she grew up with. Subconsciously, she kept repeating the cycle, seeking partners who made her feel just as unworthy.

Catherine had been in a relatively new relationship, and when she came to see me again, she was convinced that he was "the one." He was a high-profile rugby player – tall, dark, handsome and charming. Yet beneath this exterior, from what she was telling me, this man was clearly emotionally unavailable. He was grappling with the hurt of a recent breakup and was still not over his ex. Despite this glaring red flag, Catherine chose to overlook this, once again drawn to someone who couldn't give her the love and emotional security she craved, continuing to attract partners who reflected her unresolved issues.

After six months of casual dating, she felt frustrated that they still hadn't become official. While he'd met her family, she hadn't met any of his. Catherine was completely infatuated with this man and convinced herself he would eventually commit if she stayed patient and close to him. She turned herself inside out just to please him, catering to his every whim, prioritising his feelings over her own, and clinging to the hope that he'd finally see her value and come around.

She believed everything would fall into place once he'd resolved his issues, but the relationship was unfulfilling and draining. Despite this, she still tried desperately to win his approval. Listening to her, I saw how easy it is to lose ourselves when we tie our self-worth to the approval of people who, in the end, never truly value us. Catherine was constantly in fear of losing her "prize" man, and her insecurities were crippling her, keeping her awake at night, feeling nothing but anxiety and panic.

My advice was clear: If a relationship makes you feel less than, it's time to say, "Enough." You deserve a partner who values you equally. Excuses for not committing or hiding you from their life are major red flags. You have to find the courage to ask the tough questions and be clear about what you want. If someone is not meeting your needs, it's time to take care of your well-being and consider moving on.

Before seeing me, Catherine had tried advice from an online "relationship guru," hoping she could "win" his affection through manipulation. The idea that a specific text or withdrawing her attention from him for a set number of days would make him chase her was wholly unrealistic and ultimately ineffective.

Relationships don't thrive on games or tricks. True love doesn't require manipulation or a compromise of your values; real love is grounded in mutual respect, authenticity and trust. As I explained to Catherine, you shouldn't need to convince anyone to be with you. When someone genuinely cares, they make their intentions clear, show up consistently and put effort into the relationship, without exception! Quick-fix methods can't replace genuine connection and compatibility. Not only that, desperate behaviour often pushes people away.

Always remember: Trying to convince someone to love you is simply unacceptable.

The right person will be drawn to the real, confident and whole you, not a version shaped by insecurity or fear of being alone. Facing the truth in situations like this means letting go of illusions. Compromising your identity to gain approval only leads to heartache. Don't be afraid to walk away if a relationship isn't serving you fully. Meet people at their level and invest the same effort into the relationship as they do, rather than over-giving in hopes they'll see you. Instead, protect your energy and boundaries.

In our sessions, rather than teaching Catherine tricks to "win him over," I helped her see that true happiness comes from within, not from someone else. She began to understand that a healthy relationship is a partnership of equals, not a constant struggle for recognition.

As we worked together, she saw how her relentless self-sacrifice had fuelled her anxiety and caused her to neglect her own needs. Part of our work involved the following questions, which she could return to as a reminder to stay grounded whenever she felt unsure.

You might want to consider these questions too:

Am I truly happy, or am I relying on fleeting moments of happiness to justify staying?

Is this relationship healthy?

Do I feel respected and valued?

Are my needs being met?

What emotional, mental or physical benefits am I receiving, and are they enough to sustain my well-being?

Am I compromising my values to keep this relationship?

Am I sacrificing my own needs for someone else's happiness?

Am I clinging to a fantasy of what this relationship could be instead of seeing it for what it is?

Who do I need to be to feel secure in myself and my relationships, and what steps do I need to take to cultivate a sense of security and self-worth?

How would my life look if I fully accepted myself, and what do I envision for a healthy relationship?

What fears are keeping me here? Is it a fear of being alone?

Is this relationship inspiring me to grow or holding me back?

Catherine's journey was an emotional roller coaster, but it became a turning point. She realised it wasn't about coaxing someone to love her but choosing herself and trusting her instincts when something felt wrong. With this newfound clarity, she laid her cards on the table and asked him if he was ready to commit. His response was cold and dismissive; he made it clear he didn't want a relationship with her. That was the moment Catherine decided to walk away with her dignity intact. She finally got the closure she needed, and later, she learned he'd also been seeing someone else at the same time!

Catherine's path wasn't easy. She had to face painful truths and take responsibility for her enabling behaviour. But through this process, she found her voice, restored her self-respect and started to see the light. The lesson is clear: Relationships are not about sacrificing happiness for someone else or waiting for them to change – they're about choosing yourself.

The Lies We Tell Ourselves

Recognising and challenging the lies we tell ourselves in relationships to avoid confronting harsh realities tethers us to unhealthy relationships. Hoping for change instead of accepting the truth is detrimental to our personal growth and emotional well-being.

Here are some common false beliefs about love and relationships:

"I can fix him, and he'll change."

"He completes me."

"He will love me more if I try harder."

"He'll eventually see things from my perspective."

"He's only like this because of his past."

"All men are the same; I just have to accept it."

"I have to prove my worth, then he will see me."

"He will stop doing 'X' when we are married."

"He doesn't mean to hurt me. It's just the way he is; I can manage him."

"If the relationship ends, I'm a failure."

You're not a failure when a relationship ends; perhaps you simply stayed too long doing something that wasn't right for you. Remember, you are already whole and complete. Therefore, you are not half of anyone!

Affirmations can be powerful tools during this time. Consider reflecting on statements like "I am worthy of love" or "I am enough" to strengthen your self-worth.

Trust and Betrayal

We often fall into the trap of believing that we can change someone, but the reality is, you can't. This is a common mistake made by a lot of women I know. Many people convince themselves their partner will suddenly morph into Prince Charming because they think they can fix him. But you can't, and he won't! Just as there's nothing you can do to prevent someone who is determined to cheat. One of the major contributing factors to why people break up is infidelity.

If you find yourself faced with a cheating partner, understand that it's never your fault; it's entirely on them.

Experiencing rejection in relationships, especially through infidelity, shatters self-esteem. It fires an arrow straight through your heart, leading you to question your worth and wonder what is wrong with you. The answer to that is: *there's nothing wrong with you*. It's all to do with them.

Repeated Infidelity

Once is enough, but If you've ever been cheated on multiple times, the damage deepens, your confidence deteriorates and you experience another level of pain. You feel powerless, angry and frustrated. All your doubt and negativity merge into chaos, complicating matters further with added mistrust, insecurity and sadness. But when your partner refuses to take responsibility for their actions and actively covers their tracks through more lies, it becomes a form of emotional abuse.

Gaslighting

I only heard about this term a few years ago; it is used when someone manipulates you into doubting your perception of events, causing you to question your instincts and even your sanity. This distortion of the truth creates emotional turmoil, leaving your confidence and self-worth in tatters. It's a cruel form of manipulation, where the lies make you question your reality, leading you to doubt your own mind. A small part of you might think, "What if they're telling the truth?" This hope can trap you into rationalising their behaviour, and you might even find yourself trying to validate their version of events. And bingo, they have you right where they want you, questioning your worth and judgment.

Gaslighting is a betrayal that silences your voice and weakens your ability to stand up for yourself. But the hardest, and I'd say also the *harshest* part, is when you are accused of being delusional, making you feel like you're losing your mind. You must understand that their betrayal reflects their failings, *not yours*. Their infidelity and manipulation are about their flaws, not your worth. It stems from a lack of accountability and courage to address relationship issues. Instead of confronting problems honestly, they choose lies, deceit and a selfish pursuit of thrill-seeking, which will inevitably cause emotional damage.

Infidelity is undeniably one of life's most challenging experiences, where we can become engulfed in a whirlwind of negative emotions. Acknowledging these feelings is the first step toward healing. Seeking support from trusted friends or professionals and focusing on self-care can facilitate this process.

While overcoming the heartache of infidelity may be hard, it is possible to move past it with time. It's natural to feel overwhelmed by the trauma that accompanies betrayal, but eventually, reclaiming your sense of self and rebuilding your life is essential.

The path to recovery is achievable, and despite whatever you have been through or are even going through right now, it is important to process your feelings. It might feel like being swallowed by a black hole, where pain, hurt and anger consume you. It sometimes feels like one of the most devastating experiences of your life. In that moment, it may feel difficult to see a way forward but it's important to acknowledge and work through those emotions. Holding onto resentment and anger not only hampers your emotional healing but can also adversely affect you physically and mentally.

Unresolved, emotional pain from betrayal can manifest as health issues. I've seen women who have never fully recovered from the impact of infidelity, and all that toxic emotion inside can be detrimental to your overall well-being, all while ex-partners have moved on. Don't be that person. Adopt the mindset that no one can ever break you. Practising self-control and mind management is essential for survival. Forgive those who wronged you, not to absolve them, but to reclaim your peace and free yourself from the shackles of their betrayal. More importantly, this ensures they're not still in your head controlling you.

There is no true revenge. The real victory lies in moving on, respecting yourself, and embracing self-love.

Trust

Only time will reveal if you can trust someone, including your friends.

At the start of any new relationship with friends or a new partner, you won't know if they will stand by you or let you down. The key here is to trust yourself and your intuition. Believe in your ability to discern who is genuine or not. Trust that if someone betrays you, you have the strength to walk away with your head held high if that's what you decide to do. Trust that you can cope with betrayal when it presents itself and act in a way that upholds your self-respect, dignity and emotional health.

If you find yourself constantly doubting someone and wasting time worrying if you can trust them, you are squandering precious time and energy that could be better spent on yourself.

Red Flags

I've encountered women who are determined to marry someone, knowing that there are fundamental issues with their partner, believing that marriage will somehow change them. The harder we try to manipulate a situation, the worse it becomes, often unravelling in the most heartbreaking ways. Some women believe they will be "the one" to make a difference, but that is rarely the case.

Men grow up and change on their own terms, but only when they are ready. We delude ourselves into thinking that we have the power to transform them, but no one should change for anyone except themselves. I genuinely believe people can make those changes, not because they have the proverbial gun pointed at their heads, but because they *want* to.

A man might curb his behaviour for a "quiet life" as he gets older, or he might just grow up and realise that his actions are causing him grief, so he will settle down to make things easier for himself. Alternatively, he may just bury his head in the sand to avoid conflict. Trying to force and control someone is rooted in the fear that they will let you down, leading you to tighten your control to prevent this from happening, causing increased anxiety. Dedicating your time and energy to controlling your partner will result in your own suffering and will eventually increase the tension between you.

Catherine's story highlights a crucial truth: Too many women are dimming their light to please others, and this has to stop. Every one of you reading this is a beautiful human, deserving of a loving, supportive, and nurturing relationship. Cultivating a healthy relationship in which you are not constantly looking over your shoulder or fearing being let down is 100% possible when you stand in your power.

Imagine embodying complete self-worth and self-love, standing firm in the truth of who you are without needing to prove anything to anyone. Imagine how this authentic way of existing would ripple through every aspect of your life, filling it with confidence and peace. Picture the kind of partner you'll attract when you show up as the truest, most powerful version of yourself with a relationship built on mutual respect and love – not fear, tension or insecurity.

Looking back on my romantic relationships, I can now clearly see how patterns of self-doubt and fear of rejection kept resurfacing. I was always half in and half out, trying to guard myself from getting hurt, overthinking everything and bracing for the worst. I convinced myself that staying one step ahead, playing games and holding my cards close to my chest would protect me. In reality, I was following a pattern, seeking out the same unhealthy dynamics because, deep down, I believed that this was what relationships were supposed to look and feel like. It was familiar territory. I repeatedly rejected the "good guys" in favour of this psychological dance that fed a flawed belief about my real value.

Playing manipulative games only leads to disappointment, preventing genuine connections from forming. I hate to admit it, but I became rather skilled at playing these games, holding onto the misguided notion that "treat them mean, keep them keen" would sustain a man's interest. Never once did I think, "I am better than this and am worthy of love and genuine connection." This approach not only hindered authentic relationships but also sabotaged them. It reflected a lack of self-worth where I failed to recognise that I deserved better.

Never Assume Anything

I wanted to cover this because I don't know how many conversations I've had with people who second-guess their partners, trying to decode their actions, figure out their motives and understand their behaviour. Then there are the endless conversations about ex-partners, too.

Constantly assuming what the other person is doing, thinking or feeling, can drain our energy, and it is something that can be avoided entirely. It all comes down to our assumptions, which reminds me of a phrase: "Never assume anything; it will kill you."

I actually heard this line in an action film not long ago, and although it's not literally true, it speaks to how destructive assumptions can be. Of course, they don't *kill* you, but they can cause so much unnecessary suffering. And guess what? We do it to ourselves. If I hear anyone analysing someone else's actions or behaviour, I often say the same thing to them, "Never assume anything." One instance that comes to mind is a conversation I had with a friend some time ago.

She called me one morning, and the first words she said to me were, "I've had a hell of a night." Naturally, I asked if she was ok, and she replied, "Well, I was, but that bloody Mark." Right then, I knew I was there for the long haul, so I made a cup of tea, settled in and listened.

Mark was her new partner, and I happened to know him. He was a thoroughly decent man, and I liked him a lot, so I couldn't imagine what he'd done wrong. She explained that he'd arranged to take her out on Friday night, and it was now Saturday morning. Everything was going well, and she was really into him. She had made a lot of effort to look good and had gone all out with a new outfit, new shoes – the works. Then, on Friday afternoon, while she was at work, she received a text from him, saying he was really sorry but wasn't feeling well, didn't want to spread his germs, and wouldn't be able to take her out that evening.

That's when things spiralled. She stared at the message, overwhelmed with frustration and panic, mixed with anger. She'd retreated to the staff room to calm herself down.

Her exact words to me were, "He wants to break up with me, I just know it. Nothing was wrong with him the day before. This is his way of backing out." Curious, I asked how she responded to the message. She admitted by the time she replied, she wasn't in a good mood. Her response? "OK, let's hope it's not catching!" Blunt, no warmth, no kisses, nothing. She then spent the whole evening on the phone with another friend, berating him, upset and drinking wine, which only made matters worse. So, I asked her, "What proof do you have that he's lying to you?" She said none.

She'd made up this elaborate story in her head. How he was ending things, and, "Why would he do such a thing?" and how she wished she'd never clapped eyes on him – and that was without all the expletives! When I asked her if she'd sent any more messages, she said, "No, he doesn't deserve my energy!"

Wow! She'd assumed the absolute worst without any evidence, and in her mind, she'd already written him off, judged and condemned him. I told her to text him, "Hi, how are you today? I hope you're feeling better" and add a couple of kisses. Naturally, she was reluctant, but she did what I said, and he responded almost immediately. He explained he'd been up all night with a high fever and a blinding headache, but his mum had just arrived with a whole bag of goodies and was starting to feel a little better. How do you think she felt?

The truth is that assumptions are dangerous. They can distort reality, create unnecessary pain and damage relationships. This entire situation was built on a story she made up in her head, driven by fear and insecurity. If we stop assuming and start communicating, we can spare ourselves so much unnecessary suffering. The next time you're tempted to jump to conclusions, pause. Ask yourself if you have real evidence to support your thoughts. Most importantly, give people the benefit of the doubt. You might just save yourself and your relationships from unnecessary heartache.

Meet Them Where They're At

It's important to recognise that people can only engage with you – mentally and emotionally – to the extent that they engage with themselves. Their capacity for love, kindness and understanding is shaped by their self-awareness, personal experiences and emotional maturity. For example, if someone struggles with deep insecurity and low self-worth, they may find it difficult to genuinely love others. Unresolved personal issues can also hinder their ability to empathise, offer support or communicate effectively.

Consequently, they may bring their history and issues into your relationship. If they haven't learned how to handle conflict constructively, they will unlikely be able to do so with you. Similarly, if they can't be honest with themselves, they may struggle to be honest with you. Their behaviour reflects their internal state, but it never reflects your worth or the effort you invest in the relationship.

Expecting someone to behave according to your standards or emotional maturity can harm a relationship because it puts unfair pressure on the other person to meet your ideals rather than allowing them to show up as they truly are. When expectations go unspoken or are based solely on your perspective, they create a silent contract the other person never agreed to, leading to disappointment, frustration and resentment when those expectations aren't met.

Healthy relationships thrive on mutual understanding, acceptance and communication. Instead of focusing on what someone "should" do, embrace who they are and communicate your needs openly. This approach builds trust and connection while allowing both people to feel valued for who they are rather than for how well they meet another's expectations.

Understanding that people can only engage with you as deeply as they engage with themselves allows you to let go of unrealistic expectations and release the need to change or fix them. It's not about excusing harmful behaviour but about recognising that everyone is on their own path, with their own timing for growth and self-discovery.

At the same time, this perspective encourages self-reflection. Just as others are limited by their level of personal growth, so are we. It's a reminder to engage ourselves fully, to explore our depths and to show up in the world in ways that reflect the person we aspire to be. When we focus on our growth, we create healthier connections where we meet others not from a place of demand or disappointment but from a place of understanding. It's going to allow you to be less controlling, to make better choices regarding who is in your life and who isn't, and give people the freedom to be themselves.

This story highlights a disconnection between where someone wanted me to be and our mismatched emotional stages. I had reconnected with this person who I'd met in my early twenties. The problem was that I was fresh out of my divorce feeling battered and bruised, stuck in old patterns, with a mindset hell-bent on sabotaging any chance of love – something neither of us recognised at the time.

In the summer of 2015, the year my divorce was finalised, my dear friend Maggie invited me to her wedding in New York. Years beforehand, her ex-husband had played football with mine, and Maggie and I had become friends. This invitation came as I began rebuilding my life; however, emotionally, I was still processing the past few years' events. In all honesty, I was unaware of the depth of my emotional scars and the effort required to heal.

I was absolutely delighted at the prospect of seeing Maggie and meeting Barney, her soon-to-be-husband. One thing I can say for sure is that fate has a funny way of stepping in when least expected. About six months before the wedding, a familiar face popped up on Facebook under the heading "people you may know." It was someone that I'd met at the age of 21 in a London nightclub – a man I'll call Robert.

Robert was from New York, a rising star in the legal world. Eight years my senior, he was very handsome, impeccably dressed and had a deep NYC accent. We struck up a friendship during his business trip to London, and he took me to dinner. Afterwards, we kept in touch, although there were no mobile phones back then. The following year, I backpacked around the U.S. with my friend Henrietta. Our first stop was New York, where Robert picked us up from JFK airport and dropped us off at Henrietta's aunt's home in the Bronx.

The next day, he picked us up again and showed us around the city. He promptly invited us to stay at his parents' beautiful home on Long Island's waters.

Robert was a fantastic host, and his family welcomed us with open arms. For almost the entire two weeks we were there, he entertained us, taking us to dinners and parties with his friends. It was exciting and so much fun. I knew Robert was looking for something more than friendship. However, being older than me, he was ready to settle down, but at 22, I craved freedom, travel and adventure, so we parted ways and lost touch.

Fast forward 29 years, and there he was, staring up at me from my social media feed. I sent him a message to say hello, and we started chatting regularly, and our connection reignited rather quickly. As Maggie's wedding drew closer, I told him I'd be coming to NYC to attend. By this time, we'd reconnected on a much deeper level, and he offered to pick me up from the airport.

The day I arrived at JFK was incredible. As I landed, nostalgia and excitement filled my heart. I was about to witness my beautiful friend getting married, and I would reconnect with Robert after all these years. I just knew this trip was going to be very special.

When I saw Maggie at the airport, we flew into each other's arms, and I met Barney for the first time. He was absolutely lovely, and I felt incredibly happy for them both. Robert was outside waiting for me, and Barney kindly helped me with all my luggage to his car. It was a warm and heartfelt moment when I saw Robert standing there with that familiar smile. He looked as handsome as ever. We embraced and held our hug for a while, delighted to reunite, and the 29 years we'd been apart seemed to melt away instantly.

The drive to his house was easy and comfortable. We chatted and laughed along the way, catching up on our lives, divorces, children and everything in between. He took me to his beautiful house on Long Island. I felt so happy and content. Everything seemed perfect, and it just felt so right. As we strolled outside, there was beautiful sunshine. Terraces lead down to the water's edge, with a large central swimming pool glistening in the sun. He handed me a glass of champagne, and I was stunned when his eyes welled up with tears as he told me he loved me and always had. His vulnerability took my breath away as he opened his heart with such sincerity. At that moment, I realised I'd always had a piece of it. I checked with Maggie about bringing him to the wedding, and she was delighted, insisting we join them at a pre-wedding drinks party to meet everyone.

As the week unfolded, it just got better and better. Robert took a week off from his law practice, and I felt as if I was living in a dream, far removed from the uncertainties at home. He made me feel safe and happy, pouring his attention into making my trip unforgettable.

We shared romantic dinners and explored the Island on his Harley Davidson. We visited Jones Beach, ate lobster whilst sipping cocktails and slipped off to Fire Island to watch the sun go down and walk along the beach. Each passing day drew us closer. I felt like Jennifer Lopez in *Maid in Manhattan* – it seemed like a fantasy world. But more than that, I felt loved, cherished and adored. We didn't want to spend a moment apart. It was simply wonderful.

As the wedding day approached, we went as a couple, and I believed it was the beginning of a beautiful new chapter. Maggie and Barney got married on a yacht under the Brooklyn Bridge. Robert played a gorgeous rendition of *Fly Me to the Moon* on the piano, singing beautifully in his deep NYC accent, with tones reminiscent of Frank Sinatra. He even performed an Italian love song – in Italian! The day was magical, and from that moment, we became inseparable.

On our last day, he took me to lunch, and we talked about our future and how we might make it work. It was the perfect way to mark the end of my trip. But then it was time to say goodbye. He didn't want me to leave, and I didn't want to go.

On our way to the airport, we stopped by his office. Robert disappeared briefly, then returned with a mischievous grin and a ring box. Sitting beside me, he kissed my cheek and opened the box to reveal a stunning diamond ring. I was speechless. He said, "This is to seal our relationship. I love you with all my heart." We continued to talk on Zoom every day. He wanted me and my four children to move to his home in NYC! But as we discussed it, doubts started to creep in. The thought of relocating my children to another country and leaving my family behind was overwhelming. I visited him again at Christmas, but by then, I had thought of every reason why it wouldn't work. He was devastated.

Our kiss goodbye at JFK airport was our last. Those feelings of safety, trust and love he offered me felt unfamiliar and entirely out of my comfort zone. Despite everything he represented, there was no denying I was still tied to pain and struggle, unable to embrace the secure life he wanted to share with me. He had his children and a successful law practice in New York, and our lives were entrenched in our separate worlds. I wasn't even willing to consider our options, which sealed our fate.

After this, I found myself slipping back into the toxic dynamics found in unhealthy relationships, unable to break free of the destructive behaviours that had repeatedly hurt my love life. I couldn't see how deeply I was drawn to these volatile situations or their toll on my self-esteem.

The realisation was painful but essential to understanding my patterns and recognising how low I'd fallen on my own worthiness scale. Sadly, I hovered just above zero. Robert had made it too easy. He loved me deeply, but I wasn't ready to accept that it was okay to receive the love I deserved. The simplicity and sincerity of it triggered an inner conflict, leading me to resist at every turn. Without realising it, I completely sabotaged the relationship.

One invaluable lesson I've learned is that when a man truly loves you, his words align with his actions, and he'll move mountains for you. Since those days, I've come a long way in discovering the power of self-love. While it might have been too late for someone like Robert, I'm grateful for the experiences I enjoyed with him and the love he gave me, if only for a short while. I barely recognised the person I was back then, but I now understand that everything I went through was all part of a bigger picture, something I needed to learn to grow. I believe in love and know there's someone for everyone. I kept getting it wrong because I lost touch with who I am. I stopped believing in myself, my capabilities and my worth. I was blind to my disempowering habits and patterns, and now I see how easy it is to lose ourselves and how much energy and time we invest in relationships, all in the name of trying to get it right.

When Trust Is Unbreakable

I've spoken about betrayal, but now I want to share a story of trust so unshakable that it has left a lasting mark on me. It's the story of my brother Michael and his wife Sue, a testament to the power of love, resilience and devotion. My brother married his wife, Sue, when he was 21. Shortly after they married, Michael went for a routine eye test, and the optician noticed something unusual behind one of his eyes. While nothing was confirmed immediately, the uncertainty cast a shadow over their lives. As time went on, Michael's health began to decline. Further tests finally revealed the devastating diagnosis – it was multiple sclerosis. He was 22. Despite his illness, they went on to raise three wonderful children – Matt, Emma and John – and built a life together, all while the disease slowly took its toll on Michael's vitality and strength.

Watching this unfold, I learnt so much about humanity. It wasn't just the physical impact of Michael's illness that taught me; it was the strength of their bond that left the deepest impression. Their dedication and love for each other is extraordinary. Through the heartache, Sue carried their family with quiet strength and grace, standing by Michael's side every step of the way. Her love never wavered – not for a minute.

Michaels's resilience and determination to keep going, even as his illness took more from him, is quite remarkable. Sue's ability to hold everything together and dependable strength are equally awe-inspiring. Together, they faced challenges that would test anyone to their limits, but their trust in each other never faltered.

Throughout my struggles, I've often looked to Michael and Sue for perspective. Their journey has shown me that no matter how overwhelming life might seem, hope, strength and love are always within reach. How could I ever complain about my circumstances, with this as my example? I only ever saw them getting on with things, coping with whatever life threw at them; no complaints, just sheer tenacity and resilience. I'll never really know what it felt like for them, but witnessing that kind of strength made me stronger too.

Life is unpredictable, and it often throws curveballs beyond our control. Michael and Sue's story serves as a reminder of the importance of living fully, embracing the present and cherishing the people who matter most. The trust and love he and Sue have shared through decades of trials is a testament to what it truly means to be there for someone – unconditionally, and wholeheartedly. I can tell you one thing: My brother is one of the funniest people I know. We share some classic brother-sister, in-house jokes, and his humour has been his super power, which has often helped him rise above the heaviness of it all. Still, more than that, it's the strength of a loving family and the deep bonds and connections we share that I believe make up the winning combination.

Their story isn't just about illness or struggle; it's about the unbreakable bond built on trust, love, resilience and loyalty. It shows us that the right support can help us navigate tough times, even in the face of life's most difficult challenges.

Chapter 7
The Dual Pillars: Building Self-Worth and Confidence Together

*"Self-worth comes from one thing – thinking that
you are worthy."*
– Wayne Dyer.

Are you the kind of person with a vision, a plan or even a dream who feels the need to have everything perfectly aligned before taking action? If so, you're not alone. I've been there, too. I used to tell myself I needed more time – another skill, one more course, or another qualification to feel finally ready or good enough. I convinced myself I'd be ready to take that long-awaited leap of faith with more preparation.

The feeling of unworthiness is a powerful force that can stop us dead in our tracks. I know this because that was me. For the longest time, I believed that if I wasn't perfect, I wasn't worthy of success, love, happiness and certainly not of pursuing my dreams. That deep-seated feeling of inadequacy made me second-guess myself at every turn. It wasn't just rejection or failure I feared. I feared being exposed as someone who didn't quite measure up. I appeared confident and capable to everyone else, but inside, I doubted my abilities. I kept telling myself I had to be better, do better and show up better. But the truth was, I was paralysed by the belief that who I was, just as I was, would never be enough.

From my experiences, I can confidently say that waiting for the "perfect" moment is another way of standing still. There were always reasons I couldn't quite finish what I started, but deep down, I knew they were just excuses – fear of the unknown, success and judgment. It's all the same at the end of the day. Life doesn't wait for you to feel "ready." It keeps moving, but sometimes, it has a way of pushing you forward whether you're ready or not. It took my life falling apart to force me to take ownership of it. That's when I realised there is no perfect moment – only the moment you choose to start.

Unworthiness is simply a lie we tell ourselves, a story we adopt that seeps into every part of our lives. It convinces us that we need to tick every box, master every skill and have all of our ducks in a row before we can even dare to begin. But the truth is, the moment we stop waiting for permission to feel "good enough" is the moment we break free from this narrative. Change doesn't require perfection; it requires the courage to rediscover your inner truth because anything is possible when you show up as your authentic self.

Let me ask you, how often do you pause and say to yourself, "I'm worthy." Probably not that often, if at all. And what about "I love every part of me"? Probably not much, either. Self-love and self-worth are fundamental to our well-being, yet they often feel out of reach. But at the same time, do we ever practise affirming our worth? No, we do the opposite: We beat ourselves up, criticise our actions and complain about life like it's the norm. And then, we live our lives guided by this mindset.

But what is unworthiness anyway? Who and what are you not worthy of?

I'll tell you what it is: It's just a thought or a belief, both of which can be replaced. You create what unfolds in your life, and the value you place on yourself sets the tone. If you want to upgrade your self-worth, day, week and life, start now. Say "I'm worthy" a hundred times a day, and watch what happens!

Unfortunately, we live in a world obsessed with image, and many of us feel the need to alter our appearance, not simply for aesthetic pleasure but in a desperate quest for acceptance and love. Women, in particular, often believe that changing their exterior will change their inner reality, but it rarely does. We see countless individuals who have undergone cosmetic procedures and appeared more naturally beautiful in their presurgery photos, yet still struggle with feelings of inadequacy and become addicted to going under the knife.

In 2005, I chose to undergo breast augmentation, a decision that had nothing to do with unworthiness but rather personal empowerment. For as long as I can remember, I'd always wanted to have a fuller chest because I was "flat-chested," and wanted to feel more confident in my body. This choice was something I made for myself and not for anyone else. I want to acknowledge that not all plastic surgery stems from low self-esteem, even if many cases do. We must honour those who don't have the luxury of choice, such as women who undergo breast reconstruction following mastectomies or who undergo other cosmetic surgeries due to physical accidents or medical emergencies. Their journey is a striking example of resilience, and their strength should never be diminished by the notion that beauty is only about aesthetics.

When we believe that we must change our appearance to meet unrealistic beauty standards, we set ourselves up for a never-ending chase. Beauty is subjective – what one person admires, another may not. The idea that our worth is tied to our looks is misleading and dangerous, and this pressure can quietly but cruelly eat away at our self-esteem. The real issue isn't about how we look; it's about the internal belief that we're not good enough with what we have and look like. I know this feeling well – I've battled through it and come out the other side knowing that true confidence doesn't come from changing your appearance. It comes from changing the way you see yourself.

For much of my marriage, I believed that there was something fundamentally wrong with me. I failed to recognise that the real issue wasn't who I was; it was the unhealthy relationship I had with myself. I never once considered it was my inner world that needed healing. Instead, I became consumed with earning my ex-husband's approval, always wondering where I was lacking. I convinced myself that I alone was to blame for what I perceived to be his wandering eye. I felt inadequate and beat myself up relentlessly, believing that if I had been "enough," these issues wouldn't even exist.

But my efforts to "improve" myself weren't born from genuine self-discovery or personal growth. They were shallow, desperate attempts to gain my ex-husband's attention and validation, attempts that never filled the void I felt inside.

One instance in particular highlighted this dynamic. During a lunch in London, we noticed a striking young woman with a slender frame sporting a chic French crop hairstyle. Enamoured by this particular look, he remarked that it reminded him of the Hollywood actress Halle Berry, someone he'd always admired. He remarked that this style would look good on me. At that moment, my long dark hair, a defining part of my identity, suddenly felt questioned. Though I'd never considered cutting it before, his comment sparked a desire to conform to what he deemed attractive, and in an attempt to elicit a new me, a look for his approval, I decided to cut all my hair off.

The following week, I booked an appointment at the hairdresser's despite my mum's pleas to reconsider. Even on the day of the appointment, she called, begging me not to do it, hoping to talk me out of it. But by then, I was resolute and went ahead with the cut. As I watched my long hair fall to the floor, I felt immense loss. Deep down, I knew I had made a mistake and sacrificed something meaningful to pursue an impossible ideal. The reality of my decision hit hard, and it became clear that a deeper truth drove my actions. My self-esteem was literally on the floor. Something inside me changed that day, and I lost a vital part of who I was. I realised this drastic change hadn't resolved anything internal, and this sacrifice ultimately changed nothing.

The moral of this story is a reminder that true change should never come from a desire to please someone else. We risk losing our identity when we alter ourselves to seek validation or fit someone else's vision. Real growth and transformation should only ever come from within, something only we can discover, guided by our values and self-love, and never driven by desperation. It was a sad realisation for me because I knew I had made a big mistake. The deeper issue was never about him. It was about the relationship I had with myself.

Self-Worth vs. Self-Confidence

Before we proceed, it is important to discuss the difference between self-worth and self-confidence. The two are definitely connected, but they are not the same. Self-confidence is all about believing in your abilities and the skills you've developed and knowing you can tackle challenges. You could say it's a bit like a badge of achievement earned through practice, effort and success.

Take successful entrepreneurs, for example. They might exude confidence in business, making bold decisions and taking risks because they've spent years sharpening their skills. But if a major deal falls through, their business takes a financial hit or faces public criticism, that confidence can waver. That's because self-confidence, when tied to external success, is fragile. It fluctuates with wins and losses, making it unreliable as a foundation for true self-worth.

Self-worth is something entirely different. It goes much deeper. Self-worth is that unshakable belief in your value as a person, independent of what you've achieved or how others see you. It's knowing, without a doubt, that you're enough. Unlike self-confidence, self-worth doesn't waver when life gets tough. It's your internal anchor that holds you steady, no matter what's going on around you. It's that inner voice that tells you, "I matter – no matter what."

When you recognise your value, you stop allowing fear to dictate your choices. You become less tolerant of negative influences – whether it's unhealthy relationships, toxic work environments or even your own negative self-talk. Knowing your worth means standing firm, even when doubt creeps in, because your value is no longer tied to external validation. When you operate from that place of inner steadiness, life begins to reflect your worth. The world takes its cue from you. The more you honour yourself, the more others will follow suit.

So, the takeaway here is simple:

Self-confidence is external. It is performance-based and influenced by what you do and how others see you.

Self-worth is internal. It's the foundation that keeps you grounded and allows you to thrive.

Both are important, but self-worth keeps us steady when things don't always go according to plan.

Understanding the difference is crucial because it impacts every part of your life, from your relationships to your decisions. If you base your self-worth solely on external factors like achievements, opinions and status, you'll always be chasing the next thing: wealth, recognition, possessions, validation, etc. We all know these are not just ego-driven pursuits; they're hollow. No matter how much you accumulate, they will never make you happy if deep down you don't value yourself.

Let me be clear: I'm not discrediting success. Building fortunes, pursuing dreams and reaching milestones are significant and worth celebrating. Success can build self-confidence and boost self-worth and is often the result of hard work and determination. I would be the first to congratulate someone who has made good in their life, 100%.

And yes, I believe that in certain situations, money can buy happiness, but not necessarily in a material sense. Rather, having money can provide freedom, security and opportunities. Consider a family that can afford life-saving treatment for a loved one, a couple who can pay for IVF to bring a child into the world or even the simple peace of mind from knowing you can keep a roof over your head and food on the table. These things matter. They change lives.

So, the real conversation isn't about whether money can buy happiness; it's about what kind of happiness we're talking about. The fleeting satisfaction from material possessions? Or the deep, meaningful fulfilment that comes from security, freedom and the ability to support the people and causes that matter to you?

That's the difference!

High Self-Confidence & Low Self-Worth

When I was 17, I was approached by a photographer in my local town. He wanted to take pictures of me, and naturally, my mum went into full panic mode. The idea of a stranger taking photos of her daughter in his house just didn't sit well with her, so we arranged a meeting with him and his wife to make sure everything was legitimate. I was already part-time modelling for a woman who organised fashion shows for retail fashion brands at the time, but I was keen to build my portfolio.

Fast-forward a year. I had a pretty decent set of photos, so I visited three of London's top modelling agencies. I knew that at just under 5'7", I might fall short (pardon the pun). I thought I would give it a shot anyway, hoping someone might like what they saw.

My first stop was Models One Elite on Kings Road, Chelsea. I knew the area well but I was at the wrong end of the road. The agency was at World's End, and I was at Sloane Square. After waiting 20 minutes for a bus, I spotted a milk float (showing my age here!) and decided to take my chances. I asked the milkman if he was heading in my direction – a bit cheeky, I know – but to my surprise, he smiled and said, "You're in luck! Jump on and I'll take you there. I've just finished my rounds."

He dropped me off right outside the agency door. However, I hadn't checked ahead, and they only accepted walk-ins on specific days. As soon as I stepped inside, I was turned away and told to return another day. Undeterred, I moved on to the second agency on my list – Larraine Ashton, another renowned agency. A woman there glanced at my portfolio, and while she liked my photos, she told me they didn't take anyone under 5'8. Still, I soldiered on to ASKEWS, a successful agency owned by Valerie Askew, with offices in Paris and Japan.

Again, as soon as I walked through the door, I was told to come back. But as I was leaving, a man stopped me on the stairs and asked to see my portfolio. After a quick look, he asked me to wait in reception. A few minutes later, he returned and said, "Valerie liked your photos. She wants to see you." He'd insisted she take me on the books. The interview was brief; Valerie handed me the card of their official photographer and told me to get some headshots and return once they were done. I was buzzing, my perseverance had paid off and it felt like fate had handed me this amazing opportunity.

Sadly, I never returned to ASKEWS. I'd been overthinking everything and talked myself out of it, using every excuse in the book. I convinced myself that I wouldn't measure up to the other girls. I was too short; I didn't have what it took. The brutal truth? Deep down inside, I didn't feel worthy. Those thoughts and self-doubt stole my dream.

This story is the perfect example of the difference between self-confidence and self-worth. At that time, I had all the confidence in the world to walk into the offices of three of the most prestigious modelling agencies in London, determined to make my dream a reality. I didn't hesitate to put myself out there and spent months building my portfolio. When it came down to it, it wasn't my confidence that let me down; it was my self-worth.

Despite all the bravado it took to step into those offices, I honestly didn't believe I deserved the success I sought. I let doubts about my height, looks and abilities take over.

A couple of years later, after travelling around the United States, I returned home feeling unstoppable, as if I could achieve anything. There's something about the American spirit that instils a powerful sense of belief in you, and it left me feeling amazing. I decided to give modelling another go after someone I knew in the industry introduced me to a photographer in Clapham, London, named Salvatore. Together, we worked on enhancing my portfolio, and one day, he mentioned wanting to introduce me to a friend of his who had just founded a new agency in central London. That friend was Heather Mills, who would later marry Sir Paul McCartney.

Heather was young, driven, ambitious and successful. She hired me, and working for her felt like being part of one big, supportive and happy family. I was grateful for the opportunities and thrilled to finally realise a long-awaited dream.

What can we learn from my story?

1. Confidence can open doors, but self-worth determines whether you step through them. I had the courage to put myself out there, but my self-worth let me down when the opportunity arrived.

2. External validation is meaningless if you don't believe in yourself. Even when I had a golden opportunity handed to me, I doubted myself. No amount of outside approval can fill the gap that only self-worth can bridge.

3. Self-doubt will sabotage even the best opportunities. Instead of accepting my success, I questioned whether I deserved it. Without a solid foundation of self-worth, success will always feel out of reach.

4. True success starts from within. It's not about being the most confident person in the room; it's about knowing that deep in your core, you are worthy. Only then can you claim what's meant for you.

If you don't believe in your worth, no amount of confidence will ever be enough.

If this sounds like you, you might want to consider the following questions:

If I truly believed I was worthy, how would I show up differently?

What am I afraid will happen if I fully embrace my worth?

Both questions challenge you to reframe the way you see yourself.

High Self-Worth & Low Self-Confidence

This situation reminded me of someone I met at a networking event, a woman called Sophie. We'd occasionally meet for coffee with a few other women. She always breezed through the door, vibrant, chatty and energetic. Our conversations were mainly business-related, and I admired how self-assured she was. She was in her early 30s, ten years younger than her older sister, with older parents who adored her. She was kind, self-aware and knew her worth.

Sophie dreamed of starting her own beauty blog, sharing her experiences with skin problems she'd overcome as a teenager and wanted to promote her range of natural skin care products. She loved writing and knew she had something valuable to offer, and I was right behind her. But when it came to putting herself out there, her confidence was a little shaky. It wasn't that she thought she wasn't good enough, not at all. What she doubted was her ability to execute her vision successfully.

She feared being misunderstood. She feared saying the wrong thing, and even though she knew she had something meaningful to share, Sophie feared she might not articulate it in a way that would resonate with people.

Her self-worth was intact, but her self-confidence in her abilities needed work. During one of our meetings, I asked her, "'If you could guarantee no one would judge you, what would you do differently?" Without hesitation, she replied, "I'd do my first post today."

That moment made her realise something: She was stuck in "I have to feel ready" mode, but of course, all she'd been doing was making excuses. So, she decided to take small, incremental steps. Instead of overthinking everything, she committed to writing one post a week without worrying about the outcome. Ultimately, she knew she had nothing to prove. It was just a case of stepping out of her comfort zone. Each week, she stuck to her plan and created one post. As the momentum began to build, she started writing more, and the more she wrote, the more confident she became.

To her surprise, the response was overwhelmingly positive. People resonated with her content, encouraging and motivating her to become more visible. As the weeks passed, her confidence grew, and over time it caught up with her self-worth. She realised that action was the missing piece. Her worth had never been the problem, only her belief in her ability to show up.

She took action not because she suddenly became confident, but because she knew she didn't have to be perfect to be valuable. As a result of her actions, her confidence naturally followed.

Someone who knows they are worthy and valuable can still struggle with the fear of stepping into the unknown. The hesitation isn't about whether they deserve success but whether they have the skills, courage or resilience to handle what comes with it.

What can we learn from Sophie's story?

1. Inner value doesn't always manifest externally. Despite knowing her worth, Sophie struggled to express confidence outwardly. Highlighting self-worth doesn't automatically translate to self-confidence.

2. Fear of failure or judgement can paralyse even the most self-assured people. But confidence is like a muscle: the more you use it, the stronger it becomes.

3. Taking small steps is the key to growth. Sophie didn't force herself to feel confident overnight; she built it gradually, taking action one step at a time.

If you relate to Sophie, ask yourself:

Where am I holding back, not because I doubt my worth, but because I doubt my abilities?

What small step can I take today to build my confidence, even if I don't feel 100% ready?

The goal isn't to eliminate fear but to move forward despite it.

The Illusion of External Validation

To live fully and authentically, we need both self-confidence (belief in our abilities) and self-worth (belief in our value).

The contrasting scenarios of high self-confidence and low self-worth (my story) and low self-confidence and high self-worth (Sophie's story) provide powerful insights into how we view ourselves and navigate life's challenges.

We begin to see the bigger picture when we understand the interplay between self-confidence and self-worth. True fulfilment comes from nurturing both. Confidence may open doors, but those achievements can feel hollow without a deep sense of self-worth. On the other hand, self-worth keeps us grounded, but we might struggle to take the steps needed to grow without confidence. This is where self-love enters the equation. Self-love is the glue that binds confidence and worth together, creating a foundation strong enough to withstand setbacks and external pressures. When self-confidence and self-love work in harmony, self-doubt fades and we step into an unstoppable version of ourselves.

But what happens when we fall in love? Have you ever wondered how it can sometimes feel like it makes everything better?

In those moments, when love is reciprocated, it can feel like all the insecurities and doubts vanish. It's as if all of your emotional holes have healed, and suddenly, you're motivated to take better care of yourself. You go to the gym, you eat healthier, you make more effort in how you present yourself. It's almost instinctive because we want to look and feel good for the person we love. There's a rush of confidence and happiness, and it feels like maybe, just maybe, we're finally enough.

I hate to burst your bubble here, but that motivation still comes from external validation. When we're in love, it's easy to fall into the trap of doing everything to impress someone else. We push ourselves to look fitter and dress better, and sometimes we equate our partner's admiration with our own self-worth. But what happens when the relationship changes, or worse, ends? All that effort often collapses with it. If we lose a lover, that same energy and attention we were giving to our appearance or well-being can disappear, which can lead to neglect, even depression, as we struggle to make sense of why we suddenly feel lost without that external source of love.

This is why it's crucial to understand the deeper truth. While love from another person can spark positive changes, the most important love is the love you give to yourself. If we rely on someone else to feel good about ourselves, we're bound to find ourselves in cycles of highs and lows, always depending on someone else's approval to feel worthy. This is where the idea of self-love becomes vital. When you're doing it for yourself, you go to the gym, eat better and look after yourself because you love your body and respect your well-being. That's when the real transformation happens.

It's not about knowing whether you're in love with someone else; but rather, are you in love with yourself? When you act from that place, everything you do – how you care for yourself, how you eat, how you move – becomes an act of self-worth, self-respect and nourishment of the soul rather than a performance for someone else.

That's not to say you can't enjoy the rush of feeling wanted and appreciated by someone else. It's important to remember that the foundation of self-worth has to be internal. If we only feel good when someone else loves us or when we're in a relationship, we give away our power to external circumstances. When we cultivate that love and care for ourselves, relationships become a bonus, not the primary source of validation.

Even when love isn't in the picture – whether you're single, heartbroken or just focusing on yourself – your worth doesn't change. Your body, mind and spirit deserve your care and attention every day, regardless of what's happening in your love life. Realising this can move you from a place of struggle and dissatisfaction to a state of empowerment.

Unmasking Triggers: Pathways to Healing Self-Worth

Just when I thought I had it all figured out, life threw me entirely off course. Despite all the hard work, the practices and my spirituality, I found myself monumentally triggered. The pain was sharp, frustration overwhelmed me and I had this dreadful knot in my stomach. I was angry with myself because I just couldn't seem to get a grip, and that bothered me. I couldn't understand why it was hitting me so hard until I did. I didn't see it coming, but it revealed a truth I hadn't yet faced. As much as I thought I had slayed my demons, I hadn't. And while it felt awful at the time, this marked a significant turning point in my life.

At that moment, I saw it as clear as day: This was old stuff. Unresolved wounds, outdated beliefs and stagnant energy rising to the surface and masquerading as the present when it was just rubbish from the past. It wasn't the situation causing my anguish. It was everything I hadn't dealt with.

This was the day I declared war on my beliefs. They'd wreaked havoc for far too long, and I told myself, "Enough is enough. I'm done!" It felt like shedding a heavy coat, throwing it into the fire and watching it burn, along with years of self-doubt.

It was as though a lifetime of emotional baggage had finally been lifted.

Our emotional triggers serve as mirrors, reflecting areas where our self-worth has been compromised. Certain situations typically provoke such an intense reaction because they touch upon unresolved wounds or unmet emotional needs. By paying attention to them, we can identify the underlying cause of the decline in our self-esteem and deal with it.

Breaking this cycle starts with awareness. Instead of letting your emotions spiral, take note of how you react and try shifting your focus. If you feel anxiety rising, dilute the emotion by doing something that redirects your energy and grounds you in the present – like playing your favourite music, going for a walk, calling a trusted friend or even doing some housework. (Not sure if that works for everyone, but I find it rather therapeutic!) When something bothers you, like a comment, a situation or someone's behaviour, it's your first clue that something is going on for you and needs work.

When that work is complete, those same triggers won't have the same effect on you and they lose their power. You'll notice them, yes, but they won't throw you off or leave you shaken or frustrated.

The most important thing? Don't avoid your triggers. Don't push them aside or ignore them. Let them in and investigate their meaning by asking yourself:

What is this trying to show me?

What's really going on here?

What do I need right now?

What boundary is being crossed or what value is being violated?

Triggers are not there to hurt you; they're there to guide you. The moment you start paying attention to your triggers is when you begin reclaiming your worth because they reveal everything. They show up because they're seeking your attention. Maybe it's the need to feel accepted, loved, heard, validated or understood. They aren't flaws, they aren't weaknesses, they are reminders that you are human, and to be human is to experience emotions, just as we all do. Instead of spiralling into negative self-talk, see it as an opportunity to choose how you respond – pause, reflect and regain control.

In that moment, simply say, "I'm done."

Or maybe even, "Here you go again, but I'm sorry, I'm not doing this with you today."

Just like I did.

Are there still traces of the old me? Of course. But that moment marked a clear turning point, and everything changed from then on. How do I know? Because I no longer think, feel, act or react as I once did. I've gained control over my emotions, not by suppressing them, but by knowing my worth. I no longer let my past interfere with my present. Everything from before has been laid to rest. Do I still think about my past? Well, I think it would be impossible not to. But I choose my memories wisely!

Do I believe the ego fully disappears? No, I don't, but I believe we can get beyond its control and weaken its influence over us. Now, I hardly recognise the person I used to be.

A Peaceful Life, A Worthy Life

Worthiness and peace are deeply connected because when you truly believe in your worth, you stop seeking validation from the outside world. It brings inner peace. When you feel unworthy, your mind is in a constant state of striving, chasing approval, success or love to prove your value.

Understandably, this just causes us stress, anxiety and a sense of never being enough. Recognise that your worth is *inherent*, meaning it is naturally a part of you, something you were born with that doesn't need to be earned, added or proven. When you realise this, you release the need to fight for acceptance and have every right to say, "Actually, I really am worthy, because I was born that way and it is a natural part of who I am."

True peace comes from knowing that you are enough as you are. When you believe in your worth, you stop resisting life, let go of comparison and trust that you are already whole. In that space of self-acceptance, peace isn't something you have to search for; it becomes your natural state. At its core, peace is about accepting where you are without judgment or resistance. So often, we create suffering by fighting against reality, dwelling on the past or worrying about the future. But when you learn to hold space for yourself, to sit in silence, take a walk or simply concentrate on your breathing, you begin to experience what it feels like to live in the now. The more you organise your life through conscious living, the more you appreciate what is, because that's all we ever have. The past exists only as a memory, and the future is yet to unfold.

When you fully understand this, you can breathe a sigh of relief and know that your power is *always* in the present moment. Why? Because you are no longer trapped in the past, replaying old wounds, regrets or stories that don't support you. The ego, which, as you know, thrives on keeping you tied to those narratives, becomes redundant.

The present is where healing and transformation occur, and the past only holds power over you if you allow it. When you redirect your focus to the now, you reclaim control, freeing yourself to create a future that aligns with your truth.

Learning is the Lifeblood of the Soul

The beauty of life is that we never truly arrive. We are always becoming, always on a path of discovery. Each day is a fresh opportunity. A chance to grow, heal and step further into our most authentic selves. Embrace this journey not with hesitation, but with an open heart and a fearless spirit, ready to evolve and rise. Let this moment be your turning point, the one that whispers to you, "Now it's your turn. Honour who you are. Love yourself to the core." Place your hand on your heart and truly feel the depth of what you've endured to get here. Acknowledge that every challenge, every heartbreak, every battle you thought would break you has already happened. Yet here you stand; you survived it all.

Let that recognition guide you. Let it lead you to a place where you can finally surrender and declare with unwavering conviction:

"I'm done."

Done with self-doubt.

Done with fear.

Done with playing small.

Done with putting myself last.

Done with believing I'm not enough.

Life teaches us, sometimes gently, sometimes brutally, that neither the smooth nor the rocky path stays the same forever. But let me ask you something: Do you want to look back at the end of your life and think, "If only"?

Chapter 8
Echoes: Crafting a Life of Meaning by Discovering Your True Purpose

"When you love what you do, you have purpose, and when you have purpose, you have meaning."
– Marissa Peer

A reminder to live my best life is echoed every time I visit my dad in his nursing home. When I see him sitting in the lounge surrounded by other lost and lonely souls, where vibrancy once prevailed, the reality of what really matters becomes achingly clear. My dad, who nurtured hope and steadfast determination, is now trapped in the grip of Alzheimer's. His eyes, once glowing with optimism, now drift aimlessly as if searching for a way out. Yet, there are brief glimpses of his true character, a fleeting reminder of the man he once was. I hold onto the hope that, somewhere deep inside, he knows I am still here, offering my love and support as always.

My dad pushed himself relentlessly through life, but I now understand he was driven by a quiet fear and a buried resentment. He often spoke about his childhood, a time marked by pain inflicted by a cruel, cold-hearted father and a mother too afraid to intervene. The scars went beyond physical bruises, embedding themselves deep in his spirit, where love and reassurance should have been. While he found some success throughout his career in the Navy and as a police officer, his business ventures didn't always flourish. This only drove the seeds of self-doubt further into his being, even though he always appeared confident and enthusiastic. It was evident that he was haunted by inner turmoil, a nagging feeling that it would never be enough, no matter what he did.

My dad never uttered the words "I love you," which, about eight years ago, prompted me to ask him directly if he loved me, and I witnessed something instantly shift in his demeanour. The walls he'd built over the years seemed to crumble, and tears filled his eyes, something I'd never seen before. He hugged me tightly as if to say, "Thank you for asking." From that day on, he told me he loved me every time we spoke. It was initially awkward, but it soon became more natural for him. I felt as if I'd freed him from an emotional prison that had bound him all his life.

As his mind fades, that newfound freedom to express himself has vanished, leaving him vulnerable, lost in a world of fragmented memories. This once strong pillar of the community has been reduced to a shadow of the man he used to be. His sharp wit and humour are now buried beneath layers of confusion. Despite witnessing him being ravaged by this cruel illness, I am so grateful that we reconnected when I reached out to him in my early twenties. Seeing him now is a stark reminder of how fleeting life is and how much we waste on things that don't matter.

This highlights the message that to embrace love fully, we must first learn to accept and love ourselves. Self-love is a crucial foundation for discovering our true purpose, exploring where our passions lead us and where our actions reflect our deepest passions. It is what brings meaning and direction to our lives. When our hearts are open, we allow ourselves to experience the fullness of life, feeling happy, fulfilled and authentically alive.

Never Give Up On Your Dreams

Having spent 19 years in the world of football, I witnessed many women loyally supporting their footballer partners, often at the expense of their own aspirations. While some were content, others had sacrificed their careers, letting go of their ambitions because they felt their role was to prioritise their partner's success over their own. Many felt obligated to stay home, grateful for the lifestyle football provided. Being a part of that environment myself, I can confidently say that these women are the unsung heroes – resilient, strong and deserving of recognition for all they do behind the scenes.

For generations, many women dedicated their lives to serving, pleasing and striving to navigate a world predominantly shaped by men. However, times are changing. More women are finally pursuing their ambitions and taking steps toward their success. Fortunately, attitudes have undergone a profound shift. The rise of the female entrepreneur marks a significant turning point, with more women confidently stepping forward, asserting their voices and embracing their potential. I fully recognise and applaud women within and beyond the football world who have pursued and built flourishing careers independent of their partners. Their ability to carve out their own identities while maintaining their relationships and, in some cases, raising a family is something I deeply respect.

I believe we all have that dream, that longing to do, be or pursue something we've always wanted, something we know is meant for us. Yet, we often overlook that we deserve to chase our goals with the same drive and energy we invest in others. Instead, we settle into a life without it, stuck in our comfort zone, hoping our time will come one day. But it doesn't have to be that way – not when you find your purpose!

But it's not the only part of the equation. Wholeheartedly pursuing your purpose means taking action, no matter your circumstances. Life passes us by in the blink of an eye, and that quiet yearning will always linger in the background if you ignore it. That burning desire you feel to achieve your goals and aspirations won't simply fade; it will remain waiting for you to act. Don't let it become a source of regret. Step up to the plate, take control of the reins, and permit yourself to press the button on your dreams.

The time is now – not someday, not later – to pursue what you were truly put on this planet to do. When you step into your purpose, you don't just transform your life; you inspire those around you to do the same.

If you've ever doubted your capabilities, it's time to cancel those thoughts. Each of us is endowed with unique skills and talents, and it's up to you to nurture them, bring them to life and give them meaning. Discovering a purpose that truly resonates won't feel like work. Instead, it will inspire and motivate you to keep going. The possibilities are limitless, and you never know where it might lead. But if you sit there convincing yourself why you can't do it, start it or achieve it, you'll only hold yourself back, procrastinating, hoping something will change. Don't let self-doubt be the obstacle standing between you and your goals. Stand up, take charge and be the conductor of your life and the master of your destiny.

Finding Your Purpose

A purpose-driven life brings unparalleled fulfilment. Doing something that excites and motivates you is far more rewarding than being stuck in a job that leaves you uninspired and bored. Your goals, dreams and aspirations are tied to improving the quality of your life, bringing meaning and, ultimately, long-term happiness. So, why wouldn't you commit to that?

If finding your purpose feels difficult or unclear, I'm here to help you identify it. Together, we'll explore what really matters to you, aiming to clarify what you would love to create and, more importantly, *why*.

One powerful way to uncover your calling is to reframe your challenges as opportunities for growth and impact. As we often say in personal development, "Turn your mess into your message." By transforming your struggles into something meaningful, you'll find your purpose and create a life that resonates deeply with who you are and what you stand for.

Consider the inspiring journey of Jen, a young woman I'm proud to know.

While travelling in Southeast Asia with her friend Lucie, Jen experienced a life-threatening crisis. At just 22, she suffered a terrifying seizure during a car journey in a remote part of Bali. Initially misdiagnosed with salmonella, she continued with her travels, unaware of the gravity of her condition. Two months later, Jen suffered another seizure and was admitted to the hospital. An MRI scan revealed a 5 cm mass on the frontal lobe of her brain. Doctors took Lucie to one side and advised that Jen urgently needed to return to the UK for surgery.

Jen's father immediately flew out to bring her home. Once back in the UK, she was seen by a neurologist, and further scans confirmed the need for "awake" brain surgery due to the tumour's proximity to her speech centre. During the procedure, she was woken several times and instructed to recite the alphabet.

Despite the fear and uncertainty, Jen faced the ordeal with remarkable courage. She maintained a positive mindset throughout and spent time visualising a successful recovery. Just two days after her surgery, her medical team were so impressed that they discharged her. As she left the hospital, she confidently declared she'd soon be attending a Rugby match to support her beloved Harlequins, with an attitude of, "Just watch me!" True to her word, Jen attended the match just ten days later at Twickenham's Allianz Stadium, sending her doctors a photo of her with a big beaming smile and a pint of beer in hand!

In the year that followed, Jen underwent both radio and chemotherapy. Instead of letting her diagnosis beat her, she chose to embrace life to the fullest and went all out to have as much fun as possible. There was no holding our Jen back! Inspired by her journey, she launched her own podcast, "Jenuine Chit Chat," dedicated to empowering others facing hardship and proving that even the darkest experiences can fuel a purpose-filled life.

Her journey from crisis to recovery, marked by immense positivity and determination, is a powerful testament to how adversity can be transformed into strength and inspiration. Jen's courage and remarkable resilience helped her overcome her challenges and motivated her to create something meaningful and empowering. And as she aptly puts it, "You can grow through what you go through."

In late 2024, Jen received the all-clear from cancer. Her contributions show how a compelling reason to help others can carry us through our struggles. This same resilience can be seen in the incredible achievements of Paralympians, who turn their challenges into purpose and demonstrate how determination can lead to extraordinary accomplishments.

To help you discover your purpose, spend some time to reflect. Grab a piece of paper or your journal, and write your answers to the following questions:

What is my life's purpose?

How can I turn my challenges into opportunities?

What is my passion?

How can I serve others by adding value to their lives?

How can I make a living doing what I love?

If money were no concern, what would I love to do?

What is my why?

Write down your answers and let your thoughts flow freely. You might uncover something you are exceptional at or something you've never considered pursuing before but is now something you would love to explore. Keep brainstorming until you find that "sweet spot," that moment of clarity when you identify what excites and motivates you. Often, your purpose is found in what brought you joy as a child – whether it was dancing, singing, baking or any other pursuit that made you happy. Reflect on those early interests, you might just find your thing!

Next, consider how you can monetise your talents and passions, focusing on how you can contribute to society. Consider what you could do to serve yourself and others simultaneously. This approach highlights your passions and interests and inspires you to take action that could lead to something remarkable.

Embarking on the journey to discover your true calling can be a transformative experience, infusing your life with intention, fulfilment and meaning. When you understand what it is, it provides direction and inspiration, grounding you in something far greater than daily survival, preventing you from spending years drifting aimlessly along or, worse, climbing ladders that lead you to unfulfilling destinations. Instead of chasing empty goals or succumbing to societal expectations, this understanding empowers you to focus on what genuinely matters.

Research shows that living with a clear sense of direction can lead to better physical health, improved mental well-being and even a longer life. It can also reduce stress, strengthen the immune system, and promote healthier lifestyle choices. Imagine waking up every morning with a spring in your step, excited for the day ahead because you absolutely love what you do – and are getting paid for it! It's a win-win situation. So, what are you waiting for?

Jen's story shows us that when you find your purpose and commit to it, even life's toughest challenges can be transformed into tremendous opportunities. Let her journey serve as a reminder that no matter how dark things may seem, your own story has the power to light the way – for yourself and others.

A Perfect Metaphor for Life

Whilst writing this, I've had to recall many events from the past. I found myself thinking the other day about how much I miss the buzz of match day. It was always a great family day out. I remember all those times sitting in the stands watching my ex-husband play football, witnessing a whole stadium of supporters coming together, united in their passion for the game. In reflecting on those memories, I realised something meaningful:

Life isn't about standing on the sidelines and watching others take the shot. It's about getting in the game, making bold moves and giving it your all. At the end of the day, it's not about how many times you fall but how many times you get back up and keep pushing forward toward your goal.

So, I ask, "When will you step off the sidelines, stop judging others, and get out there and make your mark?" In other words, it's time to stop being a spectator in your own life. Take action instead of complaining, criticising or waiting for the perfect moment! Pursue what sets your soul on fire, even if it means risking failure or stepping outside your comfort zone. Remember – you've got to be in it to win it!

If you find yourself stuck in a role you're not too passionate about, it can drain your energy and eventually impact your well-being. On the other hand, when you go after what you love and focus on your strengths, it's transformative. It energises you and takes your life to a whole new level.

When I reflected on my childhood, I recognised several activities that brought me joy and led me to explore various career paths. Yet, something inside of me still felt incomplete. Over time, I noticed a common thread in everything I did: an instinct to care for those who felt lost, didn't fit in or were deemed outsiders. I often became the go-to person for advice, not just for my children and their friends, but also for my own friends.

It wasn't until I went on the retreat in Bali that my true calling – to serve others – became crystal clear. It felt like a missing piece finally clicking into place. Reflecting on my journey, I realise that my purpose had always been present, even in my childhood. However, as we know, life sometimes takes you far away from home, and in finding your way back, that deeper calling quietly evolves through the knowledge, wisdom and experiences you gain along the way. Self-discovery granted me this opportunity, requiring me to shed aspects of my life that didn't align with my true nature. This involved navigating through the darkness to find the light within, understanding that through suffering, we find meaning. Just as I did, in the most amazing and life-changing way.

Rest assured, when your soul's mission reveals itself, it will align with what you love, driven by a genuine desire to pursue it. Ego-driven ventures, greed or competition won't lead it. When you find it, you'll experience a renewed passion for life. Your self-worth will rise because when something comes naturally to you, it instinctively feels right.

It's perfectly normal to explore various career paths. I've done it myself, wondering why I never settled in one place for too long. Sometimes, trying different things is essential to discovering what resonates with you. This process of elimination helps identify what doesn't feel right, which guides you towards what does. To be honest, it adds more strings to your bow by exploring your options, so nothing is ever wasted. If you're dedicated to finding your purpose, exploring multiple paths is a valuable part of the process.

On the other hand, if you already know what you want, why wait? Start making plans today. Let your creative juices flow; write something down right now. It could be a single word, an idea or a plan. Remember, success is the sum of small efforts, repeated day in and day out. Consistency is king and will create results, whereas inaction will only get you to Nowhere Street.

This doesn't mean you have to quit your job immediately. Begin building momentum outside of it by doing something productive toward it every day. When you are in tune with the flow of life, opportunities will naturally begin to present themselves anyway. The first step is always the hardest. Just like I used to say to my clients when I was a PT instructor, the hardest exercise is getting out of your armchair to the gym, but once you make it through the door, you're already halfway there.

Your "Why"

Many times, particularly from a business perspective, I've been asked, "What is your 'Why'? Why are you doing this?" This question is important because your "Why" is the driving force behind everything you do. It's the motivation that keeps you moving forward when challenges arise and the compass that guides your decisions.

My Big Fat Why

Everything I do, I do for my children.

My four children inspire everything I do. They have been my greatest supporters and are the most beautiful part of my life. They are my absolute world, and I honour the incredible impact they've had on me.

Every day, I strive to be the best role model for them as well as their biggest cheerleader. I want them to grow up knowing they are enough and are capable of greatness, and that their dreams are worth pursuing. Motherhood has tested and transformed me in ways I could never have imagined. The moment I held each of my children for the first time changed me forever. The love, fear and powerful bond between parent and child are indescribable, and through nurturing my children, I've discovered they are my greatest teachers. Their strength, loyalty and capacity for unconditional love have taught me many valuable lessons. They remind me of my humanity and inspire me to be a better version of myself every single day, teaching me to love more deeply and live more fully.

What Is Your Why?

Take the time to identify what you really want and, just as importantly, why you want it. Your reason might be financial stability, a desire to spend more time with your family or the fulfilment of seeing your dreams come to life. Perhaps it's about creating a legacy for your children or simply achieving accomplishment in your work.

Whatever your reason, get curious and creative about how to make it happen. Set aside dedicated "me" time to focus on your dreams, whether creating a vision board or starting a journal to capture your thoughts and goals, taking a class to learn something new or even networking with like-minded people. You'll be amazed at how empowering it feels to start taking action. Gaining clarity on your vision and creating a roadmap can transform your path and make your dreams feel possible and entirely within reach.

When I started my business, I knew nothing about sales and marketing, and my tech skills were far from impressive. You might say I was as green as the grass, but I refused to let that stop me. I rolled up my sleeves and committed myself to learning everything I could. I didn't start as a writer, per se, but I've always loved writing. I felt I had an important message to share, so I just kept going. This process hasn't just been about mastering new skills. It's been about pushing myself to new limits and growing in ways I never imagined. Has reliving the past been mentally challenging? Absolutely. But it has also been profoundly rewarding. This journey proves that we are constantly evolving, especially as we embark on self-inquiry. It also reaffirms that you must persevere, put in the work and trust the process to create real change.

Living authentically brings a feeling of pride and fulfilment because it is driven by the heart. However, simply recognising what matters to you isn't enough – you need a clear plan, the courage to act on it and the resilience to carry it through. When you fully commit to this, it infuses your life with meaning and significance. A strong sense of purpose becomes your guide, enabling you to make choices that keep you focused and motivated.

The People Who Inspire Us

When we reflect on our journey to discovering what genuinely fulfils us, we often find that the people and connections we've encountered along the way have played a significant role. Think about those who have left a lasting impact on your life.

If you had to choose six people to sit at a table with, people who would serve as your greatest advisors, who support or inspire you the most, who would they be? They could be family members, mentors, famous people, historical figures or even people you've never met but whose wisdom and example have influenced you. They may still be here or have passed, but their legacy and lessons remain.

These individuals embody the values, life experience and expertise you need to guide you. Now imagine sitting around that table with them. Consider the following:

What would you ask them?

How would they advise you at this juncture in your life?

What words of encouragement would they offer?

What strengths or qualities do they see in you that you may overlook yourself?

If they had to give you one piece of advice to help you move forward, what would it be?

How would your life change if you fully embraced their guidance?

This exercise isn't just about admiration; it's about clarity. It's about what you can learn from the people who lift you up, those who have your back and want you to win. And most importantly, it's about taking that advice and applying it to your life.

Two people at my table would be my late grandparents, Jack and Mary. Looking back, I can see how their subtle guidance and steadfast support influenced me in ways I didn't fully appreciate at the time. These were two incredibly special people. Their quiet wisdom and strength laid a foundation for me that only became clearer as I got older.

While I've shared stories of challenges and the experiences that made me who I am, it's just as important to honour the positive influences – those who validated us, and helped us discover our light, for they are the ones who also helped shape us.

Jack and Mary instilled in me a sense of security and warmth that has carried me through life. Their belief in me continues to resonate, reminding me of the transformative power of love and the lasting impact of kindness.

I always felt a special bond with them. I connected to grandad's loving nature, and his ability to make me laugh. He was the kindest soul on earth, notwithstanding the respect he commanded when he walked into a room. His presence was undeniable. I was always in awe of him; to me, no one was like him. He was an extraordinary man.

On the other hand, my nan was tough, fearless and sharp as a tack. Her quick wit entertained us for years, often at my grandad's expense. She swore like a trooper and could deliver a punchline like a seasoned comic. She was generous, protective, kind and hardworking.

Together, they were like a double act, and their dynamic was endlessly amusing. My nan was a warrior – I remember her chasing after a man who threatened my brother one day after school, but he got away. Goodness knows what would have happened to him if she'd caught him! I was fortunate that they lived just five minutes from our house, where I spent half of my time there, just enjoying their company. Their home became my happy place, with the added bonus of a sweet shop directly opposite their house!

My nan and my grandad's deep love and care for me and my family was a comforting certainty. I often thought I'd "lucked out" to have such wonderful grandparents. They lived modestly, with no desire for grandeur, and gave so much while asking for so little in return. Their happiness came from life's simple pleasures and being surrounded by their family. I considered myself the luckiest girl in the world, convinced no one had grandparents quite like mine.

One memory stands out from those happy times: my grandad's piano. A beautiful deep mahogany piece which sat in a recess of their living room, adorned with my nan's ornaments, neatly placed on crocheted doilies. I used to pester him to play for me, as I loved how his face lit up when he sat at his beloved piano. Though, to be honest, Grandad sometimes hesitated, wary of Nan's protests about the noise disturbing the neighbours in their mid-terrace house. Still, I usually managed to win her over, and he would sit on his piano stool, belting out favourites like *Danny Boy* or *When the Saints Go Marching In*. The funny thing was, he only ever played on the black keys!

What always struck me about my grandad's piano playing was how the final note would linger in the air, reverberating around the room and leaving a lasting echo. That simple moment held a beauty that stayed with me. Years later, it took on a deeper meaning, one profoundly relatable to life.

One day, long after those childhood memories of the piano, my grandad reminded me what it meant. It wasn't through music this time but through a simple conversation. By then, my nan and my grandad had moved to the coast and were staying with my mum and Mike. That morning had been the usual whirlwind routine of getting the four children up and dressed, sorting packed lunches, making sure they had their book bags, sports gear and whatever else they needed before racing to school, hoping to make it on time. It was no mean feat! Afterwards, I made my way to Mum's house.

Grandad was sitting down to breakfast when he asked about my morning, so I casually mentioned the mayhem of the school drop-off saga. With a genuine look of surprise, he turned to me and said, "Cor blimey, have you done all that already? You're bleedin' marvellous you are."

Now, this may not seem like much to some, but to me, it was everything. Those words were like music to my ears, especially coming from someone I adored and respected so much. Grandad's recognition of my efforts, which often felt mundane and thankless, made me feel appreciated in a way I hadn't expected. I drove home that day with a smile, feeling proud and truly seen. His words stayed with me throughout the day, much like the notes from his piano that would hang in the air long after the tune had finished.

That morning sparked a huge realisation: how even the smallest words and actions can flow outward, touching others in ways we may never fully comprehend, just like a single stone dropped into a calm pond. The waves expand beyond the initial splash, just as acts of kindness, encouragement or validation can leave a lasting impact, touching people in far-reaching ways we may not even realise. Just like the ripple effect of love touches the hearts of those we invest in, resonating far beyond the moment.

Think about a time when someone said or did something that stayed with you, changed your perspective or made you feel valued. It might have been a simple compliment from a friend, a time when someone believed in you or even a small gesture of kindness. Just like the echoes of my grandad's piano, they leave a lasting impression. Planting seeds of certainty instead of doubt and sowing the seeds of worthiness. My grandad's words, though simple, carried so much weight. They validated my efforts, recognising the hard work and dedication that goes into raising a family, something I didn't even realise I needed to hear. Right there and then, I felt a sense of pride and reassurance, thinking, "If he thinks I'm doing a good job, then maybe I actually am." That brief exchange gave me a surge of confidence that stayed with me for a long time.

In this book, I explore how experiences, society and the people around us shape our beliefs. Too often, we allow negative influences or our ego to distort our self-perception. But what if we leaned into the positive influences? What if we remember the people and encounters that uplifted and validated us and showed us our worth, where we can begin to see ourselves through a more empowering lens?

Recognising and holding on to the support and encouragement of those who accept us completely is essential. Their belief in us is heartfelt and genuine, a reflection of our potential. Yet, as humans, we're hardwired to focus on the negative, which psychologists call "negativity bias," a survival mechanism that once helped our ancestors stay alert to danger. The downside of this is that negative experiences trigger stronger emotional reactions and require more mental energy, which lingers in our minds far longer than positive ones. We cling to pain longer than we hold onto praise.

Balance is important here. By leaning into the positive experiences and challenges that have made us who we are, we can consciously hold on to the love, encouragement and belief of those who see that we are worth it. In doing so, we challenge the negativity bias and kick it into touch!

So, the next time someone compliments you and says something uplifting and meaningful, accept it. Let it linger, just like the final note of a song. Let it remind you that you're capable, valued and enough. And remember, even the smallest act of kindness might be the spark someone needs to feel loved and appreciated. Let's do this for the good of all, starting with the echoes we create in each other's lives.

As you seek to uncover your purpose, approach it through the eyes of your worth. Recognise the challenges you've faced and the lessons they've taught you. They weren't just obstacles; they were bringing you closer to what you are meant to do. Reflect on the people and moments that affirmed your strengths and those who saw your potential, even when you couldn't see it yourself. These experiences offer glimpses of the real you.

Remember your council, the chosen six, the people sitting around your table. They have your back, they see you, they hear you and they believe in you. They want you to prosper, so hold on to that. Hold on to every positive influence in your life, every moment of encouragement, every lesson that has taught you something worthwhile. Go ahead and challenge the limitations that have kept you small. Surround yourself with people who elevate you, remind you of your greatness and engage in activities that align your strengths with your passion.

The lessons I have shared aren't just ideas; they are tools to help you transform your mindset, redefine your relationship with yourself and build the future you deserve.

But knowledge alone is not enough. Real change requires action. It takes perseverance, belief and a willingness to step into the unknown. Even the smallest step forward is progress. You've already overcome so much; you've faced your challenges and risen stronger, as I have. You are resilient and capable – there's absolutely no doubt about that. So, the question is:

What will you do with everything you've learned?

Will you take that next step? Will you invest in yourself and move toward the life you've always imagined? Because this isn't just the end of a book. This is the beginning of your story's next adventure.

Move forward with intention, with purpose, with confidence. This is your life, your journey.

Own it.

Conclusion

Congratulations on reaching the starting line of your new life!

The knowledge you've gathered here is only the beginning. The tools, insights and practises we've explored together are meant to be lived, breathed and woven into each new day. You've reached the end of the book, but you stand on the threshold of a brand-new chapter, ready to create a life that lights you up. Remember this always: You, the woman reading these words, are a magnificent human being. Your beautiful soul, radiant spirit and loving heart are gifts that can't be taken away from you. This is because they are who you are, and you deserve nothing less than to feel completely in love with yourself.

I now invite you to step into the boldest, brightest version of your most glorious, magnificent self. Commit to the work, embrace the discomfort that comes with growth and celebrate every small victory along the way. Let courage, self-love and unshakable belief guide your path. And when fear whispers in your ear, reminding you of past failures or doubts, stand firm.

Remind yourself that you've already taken the most important step, just by being here.

Choosing yourself marks the beginning of a profound transformation. I honour and celebrate you for all that you are and are about to become.

I've shared my journey and my story with you to highlight what it has cost me in terms of time, money, energy, relationships and love. It's been a process of connecting the dots, reflecting on where I have been and providing clarity on where I need to go to best serve my highest self.

To create the life and the relationships you want, it's essential to actively address and change the things that aren't working. Building your story on a foundation of false beliefs inadvertently shapes your current experiences. When I clung to my past, it dictated my present; the same will happen to you if you allow it. Everything you've gone through has led you to this point and made you who you are. The questions now are, "What do I need to do to move forward?" and, "Who do I need to become to reach where I want to go?"

What We Learned

This book has established that the most important relationship you will ever have is with yourself. True happiness begins with rediscovering who you are beneath the layers of self-doubt, limiting beliefs and insecurity. When you understand that your thoughts shape your reality, you hold the power to change the trajectory of your life. When you learn to become the observer of your thoughts, rather than being controlled by them and the ego mind, you reclaim your power.

You've learned that self-love is the foundation of everything. It's not just a concept; it's a deep unwavering respect for yourself. By defining your values, setting boundaries and refusing to seek validation outside yourself, you take back control of your life.

You tackled two of life's greatest teachers: rejection and failure. When you view them through the lens of growth instead of as barriers, you see them as necessary parts of life that help refine and guide you forward. Every setback is not a defeat but a redirection toward something greater.

Perhaps one of the biggest shifts in perspective came from realising that money, like everything, is energy. It responds to your beliefs, your language and your willingness to receive. You discovered that success is not about chasing – it's about aligning first, and then manifesting from that place of clarity and intention. It's not magic – it's the result of belief, inspired action and being open to all possibilities.

The most powerful revelation of all is discovering that your worth has never been up for negotiation. How freeing is it to know that you no longer have to wait for approval because you were never meant to fit into someone else's mould? You are exactly as you're meant to be, which means you don't have to minimise yourself to meet anyone else's expectations or conform to an unforgiving social trend. You learned that, while confidence may open doors, it's self-worth that gives you the courage to walk through them.

And finally, you've come to see that purpose isn't something you find, it's something you uncover. It has always been there, connected to your passions, your experiences and the way you move through life. You don't need to chase it, you simply need to trust that as you grow, learn and show up as your authentic self, your purpose reveals itself in ways you may never have expected. And when you find it, you don't just change your own life, you leave a lasting impact on others.

These lessons, combined, form a powerful roadmap to a more fulfilled, meaningful and abundant life. My hope is that I've not only inspired you but awakened something deep within you, a knowing that was always there, just waiting for you to claim it with both hands.

Understand that you were never lacking or not enough, you were simply buried beneath the weight of the stories that were never really yours to carry. You have spent years trying to prove, to please, to hold it all together. But the truth is, you don't have to fight for a place in this world – you already belong. Every single gorgeous part of you. Love was never something you had to earn and your worth has never been something to prove. You are here. And that is enough.

A Call to Action, a Time for Change

If you want change, you have to create it. Not by wishing, not by waiting, but by showing up relentlessly, with the belief that you are worthy of more. You don't need anyone's permission to live a bigger life. The only permission you need is your own, and the only thing standing between you and the life you want is the decision to start.

Now that you've seen this new way of living, you can't unsee it. With that awareness comes a responsibility to yourself to make things happen. By committing to this promise, you will uncover who you truly are and understand yourself on a deeper level. In doing so, you cultivate greater self-love. You will shine a light within you that no external circumstances can dim, no matter the challenges you face. This kind of happiness is the kind of happiness that lasts, because now you possess the life-changing tools to create the life you deserve.

Here's what I know: Every step forward, no matter how small, builds momentum. Every choice to grow, no matter how challenging, makes you stronger. The person you're becoming, the one who is disciplined, empowered and fearless – is the one who will create the results you want. And with every step, that future self will look back and thank you for having the courage to begin. It won't be easy, but nothing worth doing ever is. Growth isn't about comfort. It's about going deep within and uncovering the person who was there all along, the one who knows what they are capable of and refuses to settle for anything less.

The Path Forward

As you close this book, take a moment to reflect on the journey you've been on. Think about the lessons that resonated the most deeply within you. What truths do you now hold that you didn't before?

Write them down. Speak them aloud. Let them ground you.

Now imagine your future self: What does she look like? How does she walk through life? What has she achieved? What has she let go of?

Own your story and create your own happiness; no one else is responsible for that. Change the way you talk to yourself. After all, it's you who chooses the narrative.

Wake up each day with renewed enthusiasm and start your day with a firm affirmation of, "Today, I step into my power with grace and confidence." Be fearless. Be unapologetically you. The world is waiting for the magic only you can bring.

Let this be your wake-up call. Take ownership of your life, your choices and your happiness. You are capable of so much more than you realise, and the power to change begins with believing in yourself.

And your time? It starts now.

Your Final Reflection

I'm walking a new path now because I've transformed. I have grown, I have flourished and elevated myself. I've come to understand that access to my heart and soul is a privilege reserved only for those who truly deserve it. My space is sacred, and not everyone is welcome to enter it freely. In connecting to my inner wisdom, from the shadows into my greatness, I've mastered the art of guarding my peace. I didn't just reconnect with who I am at the core; I shifted my entire perspective, embracing a deeper sense of purpose and self-worth.

If you find me now, it's because I've chosen to let you in.

SHE IS THE STORM

She was never meant to hide or fade,
To bow her head or be afraid.
She rises up, no longer bound,
Her spirit fierce, her freedom found.

She carries stories in her soul,
Of battles fought, of dreams made whole.
Each scar she wears, a wound so deep,
A mark of strength, time won't defeat.

No chains can hold, no walls confine,
Her light within, will always shine.
She moves with power, unshaken, free,
Embracing the woman, she's meant to be.

She is the storm, the calm, the fight,
The dawn that breaks the longest night.
No longer waiting, she claims her place,
In love, in strength, in truth, in grace.

No asking, begging or seeking worth,
She's held this power since her birth.
She owns her voice, her dreams, her name,
Unshaken, fearless – no more shame.

She rises up with fire and might,
A force of nature, bold and bright.
With unyielding faith, she dares to soar,
She is enough - forever more.

About the Author

Belinda Coleman is a spirited motivational coach, speaker and certified neuro-linguistic programming (NLP) Practitioner dedicated to empowering women to discover their authentic selves and break free from limiting self-concepts.

As a single mum of four amazing children, Belinda has had anything but a conventional journey. After leaving art college at 18, her love of fitness led her into the leisure industry as a PT instructor, where she quickly climbed the ranks into management. However, her entrepreneurial spirit and creative flair led her down a different path. She began hosting gift parties and creating wedding florals, first for friends and family, and then for a local hotel. Her passion for floristry grew, and after qualifying as a florist, she partnered with a friend to open her own shop. Despite these successes, Belinda always felt a deeper calling, one that revolved around the world of personal development.

Having been married to a high-profile footballer for nearly two decades before her divorce, Belinda initially set out to write a WAGs survival guide, drawing on both her coaching expertise and personal experience in the football industry. She understands intimately the unique challenges faced by the partners of professional footballers and the intense pressures that world demands. However, she soon realised that her transformational methods resonated far beyond WAG culture – they spoke to *all* women seeking personal growth, empowerment and lasting change.

Belinda is deeply committed to equipping women with the tools to navigate their personal journeys, placing emphasis on self-love, confidence and transformation. By sharing her experiences and proven techniques through coaching, workshops and mentorship, she guides women in overcoming adversity and stepping into their true power.

Her mission is simple: to inspire women to embrace their self-worth, overcome barriers and manifest a life that aligns with their most authentic selves.

Connect with Belinda

Website: www.belindacoleman.com

Instagram: @iambel.coleman

Email: hello@belindacoleman.com

Printed in Dunstable, United Kingdom